BRITISH STEAM RAILWAYS

STEAM IN THE 1930s

VOL.
37

BEAUTY AND THE BEAST

4468 MALLARD · Q & QI CLASSES

© 2018 De Agostini UK LTD
Design and adaptation by Vespa Design and Publishing
Series consultant: Ian Mackenzie

ISBN 978-1-4439-4841-8
N1 18 01 31

Printed in the EU

CONTENTS

INTRODUCTION

———

On the 3rd July 1938 A4 Pacific *Mallard* achieved a speed of 126 mph, a world record for a steam locomotive that remains unchallenged to the present day.

In the rivalry for accelerated timings to Scotland between the LNER and LMS, this was an important promotional achievement that followed a decade and a half of development designed to produce sustainable speeds of 100 mph and more. Inspired by the streamlined diesel-electric railcar *Fliegende Hamburger* on German State Railways, Gresley reasoned that streamlining an A3 Pacific could give the LNER the edge on locomotive speeds.

Extensive testing of Plasticine models in the National Physics Laboratory's wind tunnel determined the now familiar swooping, elegant profile of this iconic class of locomotives.

Presenting a complete contrast to the stylish A4s, Oliver Bulleid's Q1 class is the ugly foil to *Mallard's* beauty. Reminiscent of a clumsily constructed child's toy, its boxy shape and harsh angles attracted a lot of negative comment when it was unveiled at Charing Cross Station in May 1942.

But handsome is as handsome does. The Q1s were designed to be powerful while at the same time light enough to travel virtually anywhere on the rail network. Weighing in at just over 51 tons, their 30,000 lb tractive effort was just what was needed to meet the urgent World War II demands for large troop and supply movements.

Two unconventional looking and distinctly different engines, but alike in their successful design for specific jobs and reflection of the creative ingenuity of two of the 20th century's most talented locomotive engineers: Sir Nigel Gresley and Oliver Bulleid.

4468 MALLARD

Finest of the streamliners

—

On 3rd July 1938, *Mallard*, the product of well over a hundred years of steam locomotive evolution and a potent symbol of the post-Depression Art Deco period, achieved an incredible 126 mph – a world record that stands unbroken to this day.

Mallard, photographed in full flight in July 1988 during its celebrated 50th anniversary tour of the UK.

Mallard *in 1988,
en route from
Scarborough
to York on the 50th
anniversary of the
126 mph record.*

W hile Nigel Gresley's *Flying Scotsman* is probably the most
familiar and best-loved British steam locomotive, his
remarkable A4 Pacific No. 4468 *Mallard* – an evolutionary
leap ahead of *Flying Scotsman's* A3 design – holds almost as cherished
a place in railway history. It is undefeated as the world record holder
for the fastest steam locomotive. However, the railway quest for
speed predates *Mallard* by at least 70 years. In the late 19th century,
the races of 1888 and 1895 between the intensely competitive East
and West Coast route companies had fired the public's imagination –
the pressure was on to achieve the shortest journey time from
London to Scotland.

NEED FOR SPEED

The race of 1895 was a clash of the titans – the East Coast train, pulled by a Stirling eight-foot single No. 668, left King's Cross on 21st August heading north on the East Coast route (comprising the Great Northern, North Eastern, and North British railways) towards York via Grantham. Eight hours, 40 minutes and 523½ miles later, and after three engine changes, the train drew into Aberdeen station – an average speed of over 60.3 mph and a record-breaking journey, owing much to the new bridges over the Forth and Tay.

But the West Coast had its own plans – the following day, a Webb compound engine hauled the train from Euston as far as Crewe. Three engine changes later the train pulled in to Aberdeen, having taken just 8 hours and 42 minutes to traverse the 539.5 miles (taking the West Coast route, which incorporated the London & North Western and the Caledonian railways' lines). Although the time was longer, this journey set a slightly higher average speed of 60.5 mph.

There were two more equally exciting races in the early years of the new century, but the Great Depression saw an end to such frivolity, and it wasn't until the 1930s that the steam locomotive entered the blocks for a new speed challenge.

The diesel powered Fliegende Hamburger, *one inspiration for Gresley's streamliners.*

GRESLEY'S A4s

Herbert Nigel Gresley's engineering achievements reached their zenith in the 1930s. His magnum opus was arguably the A4 Pacific class, of which *Mallard* is the best-known. Their design owed as much to the idealism and financial recovery of the 1930s as it did to Gresley's remarkable innovations and developments, such as the streamlined casing, wider bore steam pipes and increased boiler pressure. But there were other demands on locomotive designers: commercial air and road travel were stealing customers from the railways, and the time had come to streamline the system or face the same demise as the horse-drawn stage coach carriages of a century earlier. And, as if the threat from other modes of transport wasn't enough, another locomotive power source had been developed. In 1933, a diesel-electric engine was driving *Fliegende Hamburger* on the German State Railways to achieve speeds over 100 mph, and across the pond, *Burlington Zephyr* had managed a top speed of 112.5 mph. Gresley had travelled on *Fliegende Hamburger* and was sufficiently impressed with its styling to want to create a streamlined steam locomotive. On his return to England, he set out to secure the endorsement of the London & North Eastern Railway (LNER).

The first item on the agenda was to establish whether an existing locomotive could be modified to travel at high speeds, or whether a new design was necessary. Speed trials demonstrated that the A1 *Flying Scotsman* and A3 *Papyrus* could manage more than 100 mph, even without streamlining, and so the LNER gave permission for Gresley

THE A4 PACIFIC CLASS

Gresley's A3 Pacific class *Papyrus* (below) had proved its mettle on 3rd March 1935 by making the London to Newcastle run in under four hours. The LNER board didn't need any more persuasion and authorised Gresley to build the A4s. By the beginning of September, the first of the class, *Silver Link*, emerged from Doncaster workshops. The first four A4s had names that included 'silver': *Silver Link*, *Quicksilver*, *Silver King* and *Silver Fox*. After that, the engines were named for birds, some say after a suggestion from Gresley's daughter (although he did keep ducks). However, some names proved unsuitable and were changed to parts of the British Empire: *Dominion of Canada*, *Empire of India*, etc. The engines were a success, so much so that the 21st A4, which left the production line in 1937, and was Gresley's 100th Pacific class locomotive, was named *Sir Nigel Gresley* – 'Sir' because the designer had received a knighthood in 1936 for his outstanding work.

RIGHT

Walschaerts' valve gear, invented by Egide Walschaerts in 1844 and used by Gresley on outside cylinders. Steam (red) enters the cylinder via the valve and pushes the piston along. As the piston moves, the valve gear (orange) pushes the valve spindle back and forth, ahead of the motion of the piston.

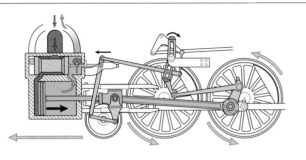

1. ECCENTRIC CRANK
2. ECCENTRIC ROD
3. EXPANSION LINK
4. RADIUS ROD
5. COMBINATION LEVER
6. UNION LINK
7. VALVE SPINDLE

Small depression *behind chimney helped direct exhaust away from driver in cross winds – this was where the thumbprint was made in the original Plasticine model.*

Double chimney *fitted with double Kylchap blast pipe. This was a key factor in Mallard's speed achievement.*

Gresley's chime whistle, *a distinctive resonant sound with three notes chiming in the key of A minor.*

Mallard *had three cylinders – two outside and one inside the frames, an arrangement common to many Gresley express locomotives, including the original A1 and A3 Pacifics.*

4498 had Walschaerts' outside valve gear *linked to Gresley's own conjugated valve gear inside the frames. The middle 'big end' bearing could run hot under the stresses of high speed running or poor maintenance.*

TECHNICAL SPECIFICATION

LNER 4468 Mallard (A4)

Wheel Arrangement: 4-6-2

Cylinders (x3): 18.5 x 26 in.

Motion: Outside: Walschaerts'

Motion: Inside: Gresley's

Piston Valves: 9 in diameter

Boiler: Max. Diameter: 6 ft 5 in

Pressure: 250 psi

Diagram No.: 107

Heating Surface: 3325.2 sq ft

Firebox: 231.2 sq ft

Superheater: 748.9 sq ft

Tubes: 1281.4 sq ft

(121 x 2.25 in)

Flues: 1063.7 sq ft

Grate Area: 41.25 sq ft

Wheels: Leading: 3 ft 2 in

Coupled: 6 ft 8 in

Trailing: 3 ft 8 in

Tender: 4 ft 2 in

Tractive Effort: 35,455 lb

(@ 85% boiler pressure)

Total Wheelbase: 60 ft 10.625 in

Engine Weight: 102 tons 19 cwt

Max. Axle Load: 22 tons

Tender (sometimes with a corridor to allow access to the carriages) could carry 8 tons of coal and 5,000 gallons of water.

Stuart Black

Fire grate area of 41.25 sq ft helped give the A4s the steam-raising capacity they needed for sustained high-speed running.

Mallard was said to be an incredibly smooth ride on the footplate.

Water scoop that was lowered to collect water on the move from a trough between the tracks.

LNER Garter Blue livery.

ABOVE
The dynamometer car showing the paper roll printer that kept a continuous record of Mallard's *speeds.*

RIGHT
Mallard's *record-breaking crew – fireman Thomas Bray (left), driver Joseph Duddington and Inspector Jenkins.*

to start development of the new A4 'Silver Jubilee' series.

Although the streamlining of the A4 was clearly of the Art Deco period, and Gresley had been inspired by the shape of the handsome Bugatti railcar, the wedge nose had a purpose. Its aerodynamics had been tested extensively in wind tunnels at the National Physical Laboratory in Teddington. Ironically, the A4 design owed some of its distinctive shape to an error. When the model was being tested at the NPL wind tunnel using French chalk to simulate smoke, it was found that, in a side wind, smoke would hit the driver's cab.

Gresley brought in Professor WE Dalby, Emeritus Professor of Engineering at London University, for guidance. However, even with this academic's input, the problem could not be solved and it seemed the A4s would require smoke-deflectors. The Plasticine model of the A4 was lifted from the wind tunnel once again, but this time someone inadvertently placed a thumb indent just behind the chimney. For some reason, the team placed the model back in the tunnel and had one final go. Amazingly, the smoke was deflected, saving the sleek lines and defining the final recognisable profile of the Gresley A4s. The shape, created by attaching a metal skin over a relatively conventional engine design, cut fuel consumption and enabled the A4s to accelerate and ride smoothly, and to easily maintain previously unachievable speeds.

On 1st October 1935, the first A4, *Silver Link*, heading up the new 'Silver Jubilee' service, pulled out of King's Cross station, heading towards Newcastle, having already broken the British speed record at 112.5 mph. Within the next year, the A4s were making the same run in around four hours. By 1937, a second service to Leeds and Bradford had been established and, thanks largely to the Gresley A4s, Britain had its first, albeit embryonic, high-speed intercity rail network.

RACE FOR POPULARITY

The A4s were fast, they were reliable, and they were safe. As a result, the King's Cross to Newcastle run flourished in the years before World War II. But the race for speed continued, and, in 1936, yet another series of tests was scheduled. *Silver Fox* driven by George Haygreen was selected for the trial and, on 27th August 1936, it set out with fare-paying passengers aboard and a dynamometer car attached to prove itself against the clock. However, due to a communication breakdown, the driver and fireman didn't prepare correctly for Stoke Bank near Grantham, Lincolnshire – the slightly inclined section of track where the speed trial was to take place – and the train only achieved 113 mph, suffering mechanical problems from being pushed so hard. But it wasn't all bad news – the LNER had established that the A4 design could pull ten carriages at high speed, and this attempt was still the fastest any passenger-carrying steam train had ever run. Almost a year later, more attempts were made: again, competition for business spurred the London, Midland & Scottish Railway (LMS) into action with William Stanier's *Coronation Scot*. This was also a streamlined design, although one on which Gresley aficionados say the skin sat less comfortably than on the A4s. *Coronation Scot* achieved 114 mph, a new record that squarely put the LNER and Gresley's noses out of joint. Within two days, their A4 *Dominion of Canada* was steaming for Stoke Bank. Sadly, it failed to reach even the previous record, topping out at a still impressive 109 mph.

LEFT
Mallard's *cab
showing the
firebox, pressure
gauges and the
driver and
fireman's seats.*

LNER'S SECRET WEAPON

Now the gloves were off – the LNER decided the business of speed trials was a serious matter and should be kept under its hat. On 3rd July 1938, a group of braking specialists from Westinghouse, the manufacturer of a dedicated brake system designed to stop the high-speed A4s, arrived for what they thought was a fairly routine test of their systems. However, once aboard, they discovered that this was to be a speed trial using the four-month-old No. 4468 *Mallard* with the new Kylchap double blast-pipe, and driven by Joseph Duddington, a man renowned for taking calculated risks and pushing engines. Two other men were in the cab – Thomas Bray, the fireman, and Locomotive Inspector Jenkins – and *Mallard* was pulling six coaches plus the

dynamometer. The brakes were tested on the outward journey, but on the return trip just beyond the Stoke Signal Box, *Mallard* started to pick up speed. By the time Stoke Bank was under the wheels at milepost 90¼, the dynamometer roll had recorded an incredible 125 mph, with a very brief peak at 126 mph. Surprisingly, Gresley himself never accepted this top speed as he felt it may have been affected by the accuracy of the dynamometer.

Unfortunately, shortly afterwards, the inside big end bearing overheated (a problem related to Gresley's conjugated valve gear) and *Mallard* had to be towed unceremoniously into King's Cross. But a world record for steam locomotives was set that has never been broken, sealing Sir Nigel Gresley's claim to fame.

SIR NIGEL GRESLEY

ABOVE

Sir Nigel Gresley.

RIGHT

The Lancashire & Yorkshire Railway Newton Heath Carriage and Wagon Works – where Gresley was Works Manager from 1900–1905, taken in 1927.

O n 19th June 1876, and deliberately moving apace as he would later in his life, Herbert Nigel Gresley opted to emerge into the world during his mother's visit to her gynaecologist in Edinburgh. This latest addition increased the number of boys in the Gresley family to five; the pride and joy of their father, the Reverend Gresley, Rector of St Peter's church in the tiny village of Netherseal in Derbyshire. After completing preparatory school in St Leonard's, Sussex, Nigel attended Marlborough College in Wiltshire, where it quickly became apparent that he had an innate talent for things mechanical and scientific – in fact, one of his mechanical drawings, made when he was just 14, hangs in the Institution of Mechanical Engineers in London.

ON THE RAILS

Gresley began his railway career at the age of 17 when he became a premium apprentice at the Crewe workshops of the London & North Western Railway as the cautious and methodical pupil of the great engineer Francis Webb. He spent another year working as a fitter on the shop floor, gaining invaluable practical experience of the workings of steam locomotives. But this ambitious young man did not linger at Crewe; the following year he moved north to Horwich to gain more experience working for the Lancashire & Yorkshire Railway. By now, although only in his early twenties, Nigel Gresley was a confident and gifted engineer and rose rapidly through the ranks, working first in the drawing office under the company's Locomotive Superintendent J F Aspinall.

In 1899, Gresley spent a year running the materials test room at Horwich before being sent to Blackpool to become Shed Foreman there, being promoted rapidly through the following years to Assistant Manager and then Works Manager at the Lancashire & Yorkshire Railway's Newton Heath Carriage Works.

By mid-1905, he had risen rapidly, at the age of 29, to become Carriage & Wagon Superintendent for the company, an amazing achievement even in an industry that was at the peak of its prosperity. Undoubtedly, all the practical experience Gresley had gained on the Lancashire & Yorkshire would stand him in good stead in later years – he had an intellectual and emotional connection with the inner workings of steam locomotives and the day-to-day problems encountered by the staff who worked with them. However, his path to promotion blocked on the LYR by relatively young seniors, he turned his eye farther afield. In the later part of 1905 he was appointed Assistant Carriage & Wagon Superintendent of the Great Northern Railway under yet another famous designer, H A Ivatt, who had also served his apprenticeship at Crewe under Francis Webb.

Although Gresley is remembered as a brilliant locomotive engineer, he made a huge contribution to the development of rolling stock before producing the designs for which he became famous. In the years following his appointment, Gresley worked closely with Ivatt in the development of coaches for both the Great Northern and East Coast Joint Stock (used between King's Cross and Edinburgh).

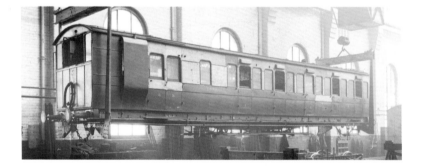

1876	1893	1899	1901	1905	1911	1918
Born, Edinburgh	Premium apprentice at Crewe	Ran materials test room at Horwich	Asst. C&W Works Mngr at Newton	Asst. C&W Supt. of GNR	GNR Locomotive C&W Supt	Built first three-cylinder loco

THE MAN BEHIND THE MACHINES

Nigel Gresley's personal life is somewhat eclipsed by his technical achievements. He was a deeply religious man, thanks to his upbringing, who met his future wife at a Bolton Assembly Ball in 1889; her name was Ethel Frances Fullagar and after three years' happy courtship the couple were married in 1901. They set up home in Newton Heath, just three miles from Manchester, and during their time there, Ethel gave birth to Roger and Violet.

When Nigel took the job with the GNR in 1905, the family moved to Doncaster, where they had another son and daughter. Ethel and Nigel provided a loving environment for their children, the family often holidaying together in Scotland or Norfolk. Nigel loved to fish, shoot, drive, play golf and tennis, and kept spaniels and ducks. Sadly, Ethel was diagnosed as terminally ill after an operation in 1929. She died in August of the same year.

When Ivatt retired in 1911 it was no surprise when the Great Northern replaced him with his young but experienced assistant. At only 32, Gresley had the background, connections and confidence to drive the company forward. His first locomotive design as Chief Mechanical Engineer was a modern two-cylinder 2–6–0 mixed traffic engine. Ten engines of the H2 class were built at Doncaster in 1912, followed by 65 with larger boilers two years later.

THE GRESLEY PACIFICS

The GNR became part of the LNER after the grouping of the 'Big Four' railways in 1923, but it was with his last engine for the old company that Gresley moved into the top rank of steam locomotive designers. His A1 Pacific No. 1470, aptly named *Great Northern*, was turned out of Doncaster Works in 1922 with a high pressure taper boiler, three cylinders and Gresley's conjugated valve gear.

A further ten Pacifics were completed after the GNR had been absorbed into the LNER, by which time Gresley had been confirmed as the new Chief Mechanical Engineer. The first of this batch of ten, No 4472, was to become one of the most famous engines in the world; its name was *Flying Scotsman*. Over the next years the class was much improved with changes to the valve gear and boilers, ultimately evolving in 1935 into the streamlined A4 class.

Gresley was knighted in 1936, and the following year the 100th Pacific to be built at Doncaster was named *Sir Nigel Gresley* in his honour. As if the tremendous publicity surrounding the introduction of the A4s wasn't enough, in 1938 one of Gresley's locomotives – *Mallard* – was to advance the class to further heights when it famously captured the world speed record for steam traction.

BEYOND THE A4s

Despite the continuing success of the A4s, Nigel Gresley was never afraid to experiment, and went on to design locomotives with radically different valve gear and boiler types. A revolutionary water-tube boilered 4–6–4 locomotive No 10000 – nicknamed the *Hush-Hush* – was completed in December 1929, although it was not deemed a success and was rebuilt in 1937. Even as CME, Gresley liked to be personally involved in testing, and could often be seen in overalls and bowler hat, stopwatch in hand, supervising tests himself.

Gresley will always be remembered for his express engines. Even though their performance deteriorated during World War II when maintenance standards could not be upheld, improvements by his successors in the post War period ensured that they continued to be the finest steam locomotives in Great Britain.

ABOVE
Engineer Francis William Webb (1836–1906), who taught Gresley and H G Ivatt at Crewe Works.

The 100th Pacific to be built at Doncaster was named Sir Nigel Gresley.

1920	1922	1923	1935	1936	1938	1941
Received the CBE	Introduced the A1 class	CME of LNER	Introduced the A4 class	Knighted	*Mallard* broke the speed record	Died, Hertford

THE LNER

'First in the World'

The London & North Eastern Railway under Sir Nigel Gresley uniquely embraced the post-Depression quest for speed, luxury and punctuality – and its outstanding streamliner express services became the epitome of contemporary rail travel.

LNER poster artwork by Frank Henry Mason, showing the Coronation speeding along the coast near Berwick.

The first railway ever to transport passengers and goods using a steam locomotive was the Stockton & Darlington, created by George Stephenson and opened on 27th September 1825. Nearly 100 years later, the S&D (in its new garb as part of the North Eastern Railway) was to be inherited by the London & North Eastern Railway (LNER), the second largest of the 'Big Four' companies that took control of Britain's railway network on 1st January 1923. Thus, the LNER could justly claim to be the 'first in the world'. It could also take pride in the remarkable loyalty, even affection, its managers displayed towards it – all the more surprising since LNER management wages were the lowest of the 'Big Four'.

THE GROUPING

Legislation to reorganise the numerous individual train operators into regional groups had been passed by Parliament in 1921; the LNER and its three counterparts, the Southern, Great Western and London Midland & Scottish, were themselves an amalgamation of the 150 or so separate companies that had previously run the railways. The LNER itself was made up of seven 'constituent companies' (including such famous names as the Great Northern and Great Central) and a host of smaller subsidiaries, and its almost 7,000 track miles (including jointly owned metals) took in the famous East Coast main line to Scotland, as well as routes to Sheffield, Liverpool, Manchester and East Anglia, and commuter trains serving London's northern and eastern suburbs.

Shortly after amalgamation it was claimed that the LNER served an incredible 80% of the urban population of the UK.

Many of the LNER's big names were drawn from the ranks of the older, smaller firms it replaced. Its first chairman, William Whitelaw (grandfather of the Thatcher-era Conservative Home Secretary and Deputy Prime Minister of the same name), had previously run the North British Railway company, while the Chief General Manager, Sir Ralph Wedgwood, was an ex-North Eastern executive, and the Chief Mechanical

Our passengers must be accommodated in an ever-increasing scale of comfort...

—

WILLIAM WHITELAW

Engineer, rising star Nigel Gresley, came from the Great Northern. The three men faced the challenge of consolidating a vast network using very limited finances; the LNER lacked the wealth and borrowing capacity of the other 'Big Four' companies, and had to fund much of its development out of its own revenues. They also had to deal with fierce competition from road transport, and constant demands from government to boost efficiency. Their response was to focus their efforts on LNER's most

LEFT
Mr William Whitelaw (right), grandfather of the famous Conservative, presents Sir Nigel Gresley with a scale model A4 at the naming of the locomotive.

LEFT
A Gresley N2 hauling a line of notoriously uncomfortable Quadarts on the LNER.

THE HOME OF GOLF
THE HOME OF GOLF

LONDON & NORTH EASTERN
OF ENGLAND RAILWAY & SCOTLAND

ABOVE
A poster by
Austin Cooper.

potentially profitable areas of operation – long-distance services and routes to holiday and 'leisure' destinations – and to attempt to increase the yield from their existing assets, which included hotels and shipping interests as well as trains. At the outset, thanks to its 1923 inheritance of several deepwater docks, the LNER had become the world's largest dock-owning railway.

One effective way of boosting income was to create a company image emphasising luxury, speed and sophistication. Whitelaw insisted that standards were improved, and within months of the LNER's launch, the company was providing Pullman trains from London to Newcastle; Pullmans were soon made available on other long-haul northern routes, and on 1st May 1928, the *Flying Scotsman* express service made its first non-stop run from King's Cross to Waverley station in Edinburgh.

PUBLICITY MACHINE

These new services attracted considerable publicity, which was skilfully maximised. Following its construction in 1923, *Flying Scotsman* had been exhibited at the Great Empire Exhibition at Wembley, attracting interest in the new, faster trains, and throughout the 1920s and '30s, extensive, stylish poster advertising extolled the virtues of the dining and sleeping cars, the skill of its staff ('discretion in mixing cocktails… regard for our passengers' eupeptic welfare – these are qualities that distinguish the LNER waiter'), and the delights of its hotels. The campaigns, featuring illustrious painters such as Austin Cooper and promotional Shredded Wheat cereal packets, were highly successful. The company's state-of-the-art engines and luxury rolling stock attracted headlines and plaudits, but some other aspects of its network were a good deal less glamorous – LNER's London commuter trains were unpopular with customers: some were made up of Quadart carriages, introduced in 1924, and described by one commentator as 'possibly some of the most uncomfortable stock ever provided for suburban passengers'. The Quadarts were often drawn by the compact N2 class 0–6–2 tank engines, designed by Gresley during his time at the GNR and sometimes used for local services in other parts of the country.

THE WAR YEARS

By the time Whitelaw stepped down as Chairman in 1938, the LNER had a firmly established reputation for engineering excellence, and a staff numbering over 175,000. Among them was Allan Richardson, a railwayman's son who started work as an office junior at Grantham loco

RIGHT
Women railway
workers on the
LNER during
World War II.

AFTER THE WAR

The post-1945 period was a depressing one for the LNER. Sir Nigel Gresley, its pioneering Chief Mechanical Engineer, had died in 1941. His successor, Edward Thompson, who had run the network effectively during the war years, lacked Gresley's flair (and, it is said, resented Gresley's advancement). Thompson retired in 1946, and was replaced by Arthur H Peppercorn, whose undoubted achievements were overshadowed by the LNER's financial difficulties and uncertainties over its future. Wartime losses and an overall decline in income made it hard to implement ambitious new projects; in Sunderland, for example, LNER executives were confronted with demands from the local council for a rebuilt station appropriate to the town's size and significance, but could only respond with generalised assurances from the Divisional Manager, C N Jenkin Jones, that 'the company has the interests of Sunderland at heart and there is no suggestion that the town is being put off the map'.

LEFT
Pullman carriages arrived in Britain from America after the 1873 agreement between George Mortimer Pullman and the Midland Railway.

INSET
Barber's chair on a Pullman carriage.

shed in 1937, and later worked as an engine cleaner before eventually becoming a driver. In an interview for a recent BBC documentary, he describes the prevailing atmosphere as 'Dickensian... the loco superintendent was one step down from God', and remembers long, gruelling shifts in which 'you were soaked in rags of paraffin from rubbing the engine down'. But life was to become harder with the coming of World War II in 1939. A few days before its outbreak, the passage of the Emergency Powers (Defence) Act led to the withdrawal of many high-speed and luxury services, and the introduction of a Railway Executive Committee responsible to the government for the operation of all four networks. It was chaired by Sir Ralph Wedgwood, who handed over the General Managership of LNER to Sir Charles Newton.

Wartime conditions included the imposition of blackout conditions on passenger trains and shortages of commodities such as high-quality coal. However, the War also led to positive developments, such as the employment of more than 100,000 women in railway jobs that were formerly an exclusively male preserve.

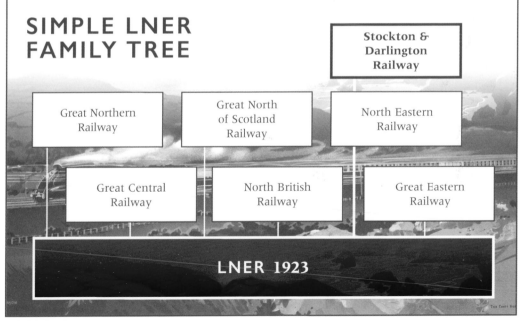

SIMPLE LNER FAMILY TREE

		Stockton & Darlington Railway
Great Northern Railway	Great North of Scotland Railway	North Eastern Railway
Great Central Railway	North British Railway	Great Eastern Railway

LNER 1923

These proposals came to nothing, and plans for the new Labour government to nationalise the entire rail system were strengthened by LNER Chairman Sir Ronald Matthews' statement, quoted in Paul Smith's article *The Exploiter and the Exploited*, that his network 'would be financially unable to continue to operate on its own, and in the interests of its shareholders could not oppose a takeover by the state'. Nationalisation took place in January 1948 with the creation of British Railways, whose Eastern, North Eastern and Scottish regions took over the LNER's infrastructure.

WHERE IS SHE NOW?

After her 1988 runs, *Mallard* returned home to the National Railway Museum, York **(www.nrm.org.uk),** where she is the centrepiece of the permanent steam exhibition.

LNER ROUTES

The LNER's main line services included routes from London to Edinburgh and Glasgow, via Peterborough, Grantham, Doncaster, York, Durham and Newcastle; it also operated on the former Great North of Scotland tracks from Edinburgh to Aberdeen and Keith, and west to Fort William and Mallaig.

In England, its trains ran via Leicester and Nottingham to Sheffield, and on to Manchester and Liverpool, and it served major centres such as Leeds, as well as numerous towns and cities throughout eastern England, among them Cambridge, Lincoln, Colchester, Ipswich, Harwich, Norwich and Great Yarmouth. It also ran laterally, with lines from Leeds through York and Selby to Hull, and colliery tracks running from Durham and Northumberland pits to the ports on the north-east coast. Today, most of its former lines are worked by GNER, One, ScotRail, Arriva Trains Northern, and Central.

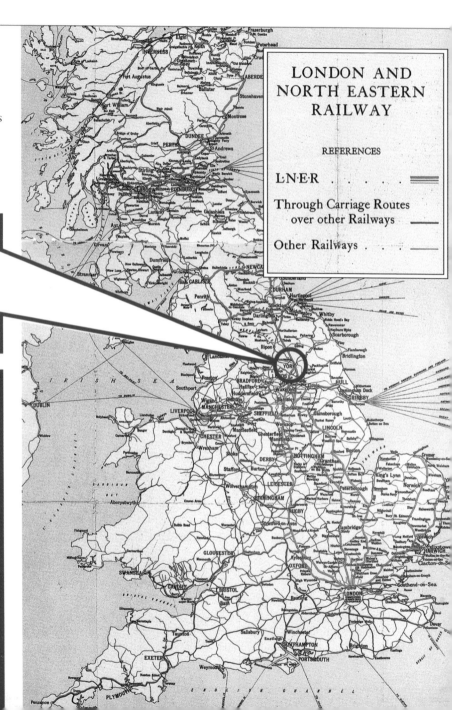

LONDON AND NORTH EASTERN RAILWAY

REFERENCES

L·N·E·R . . . . .

Through Carriage Routes over other Railways

Other Railways . . .

CONNECTION TO THE NORTH

The LNER's primary terminal

King's Cross station, the hub of the LNER route to the north, was built in 1852 for the GNR, but was overwhelmed with the increasing demands from rail traffic; a problem that also faced the LNER with high-speed trains running on old tracks.

Queen Victoria's entourage arriving at King's Cross station to travel to York Races, circa 1870.

From the day it opened, the two glazed arches of the King's Cross facade – built because the station was designed in two halves for departures and arrivals and divided by an Italianate clock tower – had a dramatic impact on the mid-19th century traveller. The design of the station elicited a broad gamut of responses from both rail travellers and rail workers. But, from the rail worker's perspective, the station had inherent flaws: despite being the largest station in England, the layout was cramped, there was a bottleneck just beyond the platforms, and unusually narrow train sheds caused severe operational difficulties.

The arches (just visible in the background) of the riding school of the Russian Czars inspired the design of King's Cross.

THE FIRST STONES

The process of commissioning and building the London terminal of the Great Northern Railway began with the London & York Railway Bill, which received Royal Assent in 1846. This procedure was led by Edward Dennison, parliamentary counsel for the GNR and son of Lord Grimthorpe, GNR Chairman from 1847–64 (both his brothers were also Directors).

In 1850, four years after the Bill was passed, the construction of the track entered London with the building of the main line from Peterborough to a temporary station at Maiden Lane. However, it would take two more years to build the Gas Works and Copenhagen tunnels to enable rail access to the site of the new King's Cross station, a process made particularly onerous because tunnelling had to pass under the Regent's Canal. These same problems re-emerged with the station's extension for the new Channel Tunnel Rail Link which opened in 2007.

LEWIS CUBITT

The architect of King's Cross, Lewis Cubitt (1799–1883), was commissioned by the GNR to create a new London terminus to serve Yorkshire, the north east and Scotland. Like Dennison, Cubitt was no stranger to the railways: his older brother Thomas, a leading master builder in London, worked on the King's Cross project as an engineer; his uncle, Sir William Cubitt, and cousin, Joseph, were both engineers for the GNR, and his uncle Benjamin was the first locomotive superintendent of the Great Northern.

The structure was built between 1850 and 1852 on the site of the expanded London smallpox and fever hospital by John and William Jay of the Euston Road. At the time, this area was known as 'Battle Bridge' – according to some, the site of Boudicca's final battle and where her

body lies, supposedly under Platform 8. The station took its name from a 60 ft monument to George IV, erected in the 1830s, but demolished within ten years as it was deemed cheap and vulgar.

The opening of King's Cross took place on 14th October 1852, in very different surroundings from those seen today. By the early 1850s, this area of London was a site of growing industrialisation. The Imperial Gas Works was already open and the area contained a number of brick fields and kilns. Houses and new roads were also being built out into the open country to the north of the station.

Despite providing huge 150,000 gallon water tanks on the top level, a six-storey granary that could hold 60,000 sacks, room for 15,200 tons of coal and stabling for 300 horses, King's Cross was almost immediately overloaded. The two tunnels – Gas Works and Copenhagen – were close to the platforms and quickly became a bottleneck. The area above the tunnels, known as Belle Isle, rapidly turned into a hell on earth amidst the constant soot and cinders. Also, the notorious Hotel Curve was particularly tricky to navigate – one train even slipped backwards,

DeAGOSTINI PRESENTS

AN AMAZING NEW BOOK SERIES

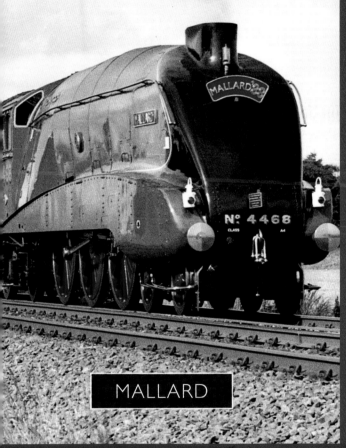

MALLARD

FLYING SCOTSMAN

ROCKET

BRITISH STEAM RAILWAYS

WELCOME TO
BRITISH STEAM RAILWAYS

This amazing new book series chronicles the triumphs of British steam, from the ingenious engineers who laid the foundations for the railways to the industrial boom of the Victorian Era and the ground-breaking innovations of the 20th century. Each book in this series investigates the locomotives, engineering breakthroughs and celebrated railway lines that helped build modern Britain.

THE BRITISH STEAM RAILWAYS BOOK SERIES

This series of lavishly-illustrated hardcover volumes provides a comprehensive history of British steam railways, divided into five eras:

- WORLD WAR II & POSTWAR BRITAIN
- STEAM IN THE 1930s
- WORLD WAR I & THE 1920s
- LATE VICTORIAN & EDWARDIAN ERAS
- THE DAWN OF STEAM

PLUS...

- LEGENDARY RAILWAY COMPANIES

These five special volumes provide a detailed history of the four regional companies created by the Grouping in 1923: the LMS, LNER, GWR and the Southern - and the single company, British Railways established by nationalisation of the entire network in 1948.

FAMOUS LOCOMOTIVES
A history of the legendary locomotives that powered Britain during the Age of Steam. Each featured locomotive is illustrated in painstaking detail by expert artists.

GREAT BRITISH RAILWAYS
The fascinating history of the railway companies, small and large, that reshaped the nation, eventually creating a rail network of over 20,000 miles.

WHO'S WHO
Profiles of the most famous engineers and inventors of the Age of Steam, including George Stephenson and Sir Nigel Gresley.

ENGINEERING FEATS
The creation of Britain's rail infrastructure.

WORKING ON THE RAILWAYS
Real-life stories of the men and women who built and ran the railways.

THE STORY OF STEAM
A series of articles chronicling the history of steam power, from ancient inventors to the modern day.

BRITISH STEAM RAILWAYS BOOST PICTURE CREDITS
AKG Images: 2br; Alamy: cover L, cover C; Graham Howden/Cordaiy Photo Library Ltd: 6 main; Michael Morant: 6bl; Milepost 92 ½: 3bl, 5 main; Rex Features: 2 4th r; Science & Society Picture Library: National Railway Museum: cover R, 2 2nd r, 3rd r & 5th r, 3 main, 4 main & bl, 5bl, 7 main, bc; WA Sharman/Milepost 92½: 7 main.

THE DAWN OF STEAM

In the early 19th century, British inventors and engineers, including Richard Trevithick and George Stephenson turned the steam engine into a source of motive power – and changed the world forever. This period saw the development of the technologies necessary for railways, and the foundation of the Stockton & Darlington railway, the Liverpool & Manchester and Great Western Railway companies.

Locomotion No 1

Rocket

FEATURED LOCOMOTIVES INCLUDE:

- S&DR *Locomotion No 1*
- L&MR Stephenson's *Rocket*
- L&MR *Lion*
- GWR *Fireflies*
- Ffestiniog Railway's Fairlies
- GWR *Iron Duke*
- LB&SCR Terrier Tanks
- CR Single No 123

LATE VICTORIAN & EDWARDIAN ERAS

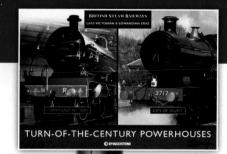

TURN-OF-THE-CENTURY POWERHOUSES

The 1850s saw the beginning of a golden age of steam, with the railways becoming a vital part of Britain's economy and both passenger and freight transport becoming big business. As rival rail companies engaged in cut-throat competition, complex timetabling and standardised time became a necessity, while the Tay Bridge disaster emphasised the need for much more rigorous engineering and construction standards.

Midland Compound No. 1000

FEATURED LOCOMOTIVES INCLUDE:

- LNWR Jumbos
- LSWR Adams O2 Tanks
- GER J15
- HR Jones Goods 4-6-0

- CR Dunalastair class
- MR Compound No 1000
- GWR *City of Truro*
- The Atlantic 4-4-2 classes

City of Truro

WORLD WAR I & THE 1920s

With the turn of the 19th century, designers such as G J Churchward and H A Ivatt established new standards of design and production excellence to create a generation of the big powerful engines required to haul increasingly heavy passenger and freight trains.

Nationalisation of the rail network during World War I underlined the unnecessary costs and duplication of myriad railway companies competing for business. Rather than retaining a nationalised network, Parliament compromised with an Act of Parliament that combined all existing companies into four new geographically determined private companies: the so-called 'Big Four'.

Castle Class

FEATURED LOCOMOTIVES INCLUDE:

- GER B12 4-6-0
- SR Maunsell Moguls
- LNER *Flying Scotsman*
- SR King Arthur class
- GWR Caste Class
- LMS Royal Scot class
- GWR *King George V*
- SR Lord Nelson class

Flying Scotsman

STEAM IN THE 1930s

BEAUTY AND THE BEAST

The 1930s marked a period of standardisation and regulation, with the 'Big Four' railway companies introducing new modernised classes and even working to push the limits of locomotive design with streamlined creations like the legendary *Mallard*. Britain's modern railway system was to prove an asset in the looming conflict of World War II.

The Q and Q1 Classes

FEATURED LOCOMOTIVES INCLUDE:

- LNER A4 Pacific *Mallard*
- LMS Pacific *Princess Elizabeth*
- SR Schools class
- LNER *Green Arrow* No 4771
- GWR 14XX Auto Tanks
- LMS Duchess Pacifics
- GWR Dukedog class
- LMS The Black 5s

City of Truro

WORLD WAR II & POSTWAR BRITAIN

END OF AN ERA

World War II was a baptism of fire for the railways, with locomotives ferrying urgently required war material and engineers constantly repairing damage caused by German air raids. The end of the war in 1945 also brought nationalisation of the railways, upgraded engines and a variety of new steam locomotive designs. Although the switch to electrification and diesel locomotives ultimately marked the twilight of steam, many legendary locomotives are preserved for future generations.

Duke of Gloucester

Duke of Gloucester

FEATURED LOCOMOTIVES INCLUDE:

- LNER B1 4-6-0s
- War Dept J94 Austerities
- SR Merchant Navy class *Clan Line*
- SR Bulleid's Light Pacifics

- LNER The Peppercorn A/A2 Pacifics
- LMS Ivatt's 2-6-0 and 2-6-2 Tanks
- BR Britannia class Pacifics
- BR 9F class *Evening Star*

Evening Star

The series includes five special volumes chronicling the history of Britain's best-known 20th-century railway companies, including the 'Big Four' created by the Grouping in 1923:

LEGENDARY RAILWAY COMPANIES VOLUMES ARE:

- The London, Midland and Scottish Railway
- The London and North Eastern Railway
- The Great Western Railway
- The Southern Railway

and the company established to take over the entire rail network on nationalisation in 1948:

- British Railways.

British Steam Railways concludes with a complete index to the entire series.

BRITISH STEAM RAILWAYS

DEAGOSTINI.CO.UK/STEAMRAILWAYS

DeAGOSTINI

unbeknown to its crew amidst the smoke and grime, until it crashed into the train directly behind.

The station complex grew rapidly with the addition of the engine shed (later known as 'Top Shed') and the massive coal and goods depots. The GNR management had predicted growth in coal, meat and vegetable traffic for the burgeoning city of London, but was unprepared for how quickly this expansion took place. By 1900, the King's Cross goods depot was receiving over one million tons of goods per year (excluding coal and cattle, which were handled by different depots at the station). A potato market soon sprung up on York Way above the main Gas Works Tunnel. Unloading took place at a series of purpose-built warehouses on the eastern side of the goods station, but could not keep up with the increasing traffic – at the height of the period, there would often be more than a thousand potato wagons waiting in and around King's Cross station!

Regardless of its operational difficulties, King's Cross flourished, becoming one of the UK's most recognisable and famous stations. Today, the advent of electrification, the closure of the link lines to the Metropolitan, improvements to the track and driving van trailers have virtually eliminated the problems of bottlenecks and inclines. Currently the station hosts upwards of 40 million passengers a year, and a significantly cleaner image has been portrayed in recent films, such as *Harry Potter and the Philosopher's Stone*.

HIGH-SPEED RUNNING

The running of high-speed trains, such as the *Silver Jubilee* and the *Elizabethan*, from King's Cross posed a number of challenges on the East Coast main line. The inadequacy of the track first became a major concern during a publicity run from King's Cross on 27th September 1935. Hauled by *Silver Link*, the train carried LNER officers, invited guests and the press. The crew was told to 'let her go and see what she can do'. As the train crossed the points at Grantham station, a series of jolts rattled the carriages. In Sir Nigel Gresley's compartment was the LNER's Chief Civil Engineer, Mr Chas J Brown, who was less than happy with the bumps. Unlike the ride in the coaches, *Silver*

Silver Link *photographed at* King's Cross by F E Fox in 1938.

Link's footplate was deceptively smooth, so much so that the crew continued to drive at high speed until Gresley climbed through the tender corridor and told them to slow down. Although a new British record of 112 mph had been set, driver Taylor thought they had been running at only 90 mph!

One of the reasons for the rough ride was the suspension on Gresley's coaches. Sudden track transitions caused the springs to compress to their limits then rebound with a sharp jolt. Despite the unease between Gresley and Brown on the trial run, both quickly took steps to solve the problems. Gresley modified the coach springs, whilst Brown initiated a series of track improvements. For high-speed running, there were three problems with the track; most of the sideways jolts were caused by insufficient or non-existent 'easements'. Easements are smooth transitions from straight track to curved track, which for higher speed running, should be long and smooth. The theory of easements was well understood in the 1930s, but the LNER was still in the process of aligning its track to incorporate high-speed easements.

LEFT
LNER Southern Area Superintendent, M Barrington-Ward.

Another problem was the 'super-elevation', also known as 'cant'. This is where the track is tilted slightly towards the centre of a curve to lessen the outward centrifugal forces acting on the train. In the early 1930s, the East Coast main line curves were only super-elevated for comfortable running up to 80–85 mph. A third problem was the age and type of rail in use. *Mallard's* famous 126 mph record passed over a series of 40 ft rails laid in 1910 that actually had a strict 90 mph speed limit! The LNER made regular improvements to the permanent way but the costs were astronomical – the annual materials used amounted to as much as 60,000 tons of rails, 1¼ million sleepers and about half a million cubic yards of ballast.

As well as technical problems, there were other difficulties, the most serious of which was the separation of trains. Even though the A4s were fitted with the best vacuum brakes, their stopping distances were

We could easily have gone faster if we had wanted to – we were not out by any means…

DRIVER TAYLOR OF THE *SILVER LINK*
112 MPH RECORD RUN

greater. A number of schemes were considered, including the addition of signals to give earlier warnings. Another plan was to increase the separation distance between the signals. Both these proposals were considered too expensive, so a system of 'double blocking' was instigated in areas with semaphore signals. This system doubled the spacing between fast trains by waiting for the train in front to clear an extra set of signals.

The final challenge to running high-speed services was timetabling. The East Coast main line was already congested with passenger, commuter, freight and heavy coal trains. These represented a range of speeds, and were already very difficult to timetable. The problem was summed up by the Superintendent of the LNER's Southern Area, V M

THE LADYKILLERS

A recently remade and relocated Ealing Studios black comedy set in an even blacker location, *The Ladykillers* portrays smoggy London at its stereotypical worst. The smoke and noise at Belle Isle was perfect for the setting, where a seemingly befuddled landlady, Mrs Wilberforce, (brilliantly played by Katie Johnson) becomes the recipient of £60,000 stolen in a robbery masterminded by her tenant, Professor Marcus (brilliantly portrayed by Alec Guinness).

Marcus's gang, posing as musicians, carry out the robbery successfully, but their plot is discovered by Mrs Wilberforce. The gang decide that they need to murder her but she has no intention of dying and, one by one, the gang members mysteriously wind up killing themselves off, obscured by the smoke and noise of the locomotives, the last being killed by a knock on the head from a railway signal. Mrs Wilberforce and her parrot carry on regardless.

Barrington-Ward in an address to the Institute of Transport in 1937:
'a high-speed train may perform an excellent service to the public and
prove a good advertisement to the railway, but from an operating point
of view its effect on other trains is liable to be serious, and of course to
the timetable clerk the nearer all trains run to the same speed the
better'. Great skill was required to arrange these timetables, and it was
possible to divert slower trains on to secondary lines. The problem was
also eased in places by adding new passing sidings and loops for slower
trains, and by upgrading sections of the track to four lines. Both proved
expensive, and even today much of the East Coast main line is still
double track.

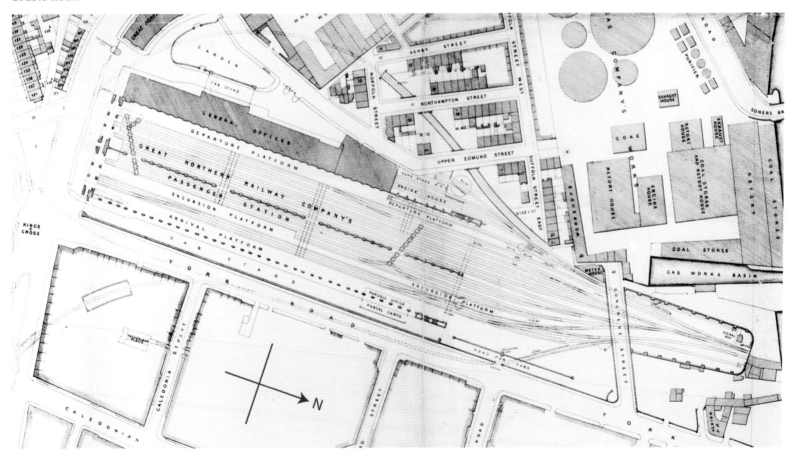

LEFT
*A map of King's
Cross station,
showing the track
bottleneck under
the Regent's Canal
and the branches
to the Metropolitan
widened lines.*

MEN AT WORK

'There comes a crowd of burly navvies...'

GEORGE ELIOT

Most people know the names of the great Victorian railway engineers, such as Brunel and Stephenson... but who remembers the 'navvies' – that extraordinary band of men who dug the cuttings, blasted the tunnels and created the embankments on which we still travel today?

Navvies around 1904, building the Piccadilly Underground.

The world has received a new impulse. The genius of the age, like a mighty river of the new world, flows onward, full, rapid, and irresistible'. So said Henry Booth, in 1830 – the year in which the Liverpool & Manchester Railway (of which Booth was treasurer) opened. The Liverpool and Manchester was the first main line railway designed to carry both goods and passengers, and Booth's words proved to be prophetic indeed: the coming of the railway was to play a crucial role in transforming Britain into the world's leading industrial nation.

BUILDING THE FUTURE

There were two great periods of railway building in Britain. The first occurred in the 1830s, when the London & Birmingham and the Great Western railways were constructed (the GWR main line to Bristol was fully completed in 1841); the second was in the mid- to late 1840s. Given the resources – human muscle power – growth took place at an astonishing pace: in 1830, there were less than 100 miles of railway; by 1840, nearly 1,500 miles; by the end of 1850, some 6,000 miles were open for traffic and, by 1860, most of Britain's main lines had been built. By 1875, with the opening of the Midland's Settle & Carlisle line, all of the main lines (except the Great Central), and most of the secondary lines, had been completed. A national rail system had been created in less than 50 years. This was an amazing achievement, especially given that it was all done by hand – by 'navvies' – vast gangs of navvies, using nothing more than picks, shovels and explosives.

In 1846–7, the height of the 'railway mania' years, there were an estimated 200,000 navvies at work on the 3,000-or so miles of new line under construction in Britain at the time; the number of navvies employed would never again reach this level. The first navvies came from the gangs who had built the canals (thus the name 'navigators') and roads. Later, they arrived from the Fens, whose 'bankers' had built the sea walls of that area, and from Ireland, Scotland, and the dales of Yorkshire and Lancashire.

From early on they were recognised as being a special breed of men – and regarded themselves as such, too. They advertised their difference in their distinctive, colourful clothing and were proud of their ability to out-work – and out-drink – the common labourer.

RANDIES AND RELIGION

Navvies worked hard, and when pay day finally came around they made the most of it, with drunken parties called 'randies' that lasted until the cash ran out. Riots often started over religious differences, usually with Protestant navvies attacking Catholic Irish. One infamous riot occurred at Penmaenmawr in 1846, when 300 Welsh navvies drove away Irish navvies working on the line. Such confrontations were frequent and with randies and the immoral goings-on in the shanty towns, the general view was that navvies were a sinful lot. Despite this, in the mid-19th century, few efforts were made to save their souls. However, in 1878, Elizabeth Garnett published her first Quarterly Letter to Navvies, which began to win an audience once Garnett included material of more interest to he men, such as lists of works, deaths and marriages.

Below is an extract from an abstinence song distributed in the 1880s by other equally zealous missionary ladies:

Yes, I'm an English navvy; but, oh, not an English sot, I have run my pick through alcohol, in bottle, glass or pot, And with the spade of abstinence, and all the power I can I am spreading out a better road for every working man.'

BLOOD AND SWEAT

Most of the navvies' work involved creating embankments, making cuttings, and tunnelling (bridges and viaducts were built in some cases by the railway company, or more usually by the principal contractor, using their own specialist workers). Embankments were the easiest of the three to work on, and usually involved carting soil from a nearby cutting. Light rails were laid and trucks filled with earth were pulled by horses at increasing speed towards the embankment edge. At the last minute, the horse was released and the truck continued until it hit a large piece of wood laid across the end of the track, at which point it tipped its contents over the edge, inching the embankment forward at a steady pace hour by hour. Making cuttings was more of a challenge. All the excavation was done by hand; if the soil was needed for a nearby embankment, it was loaded on to trucks and hauled away to be tipped. If not, the earth had to be lifted to the top of the cutting and dumped at the top by means of 'barrow runs' up the sides of the cutting. It was arduous and dangerous work: unless the horse pulling the barrow up the side worked in harmony with the navvy doing the steering, horse, barrow or both could fall off the narrow plank – on to the navvy, with serious results. If the cutting had to be blasted through rock, the dangers of injury from falling fragments of stone or from poorly controlled explosions in confined spaces can be imagined.

> ## The females were corrupted, many of them, and went away with the men, and lived amongst them in habits that civilized language will hardly allow a description of.
>
> ROBERT RAWLINSON, QUOTED IN COLEMAN'S *THE RAILWAY NAVVIES*.

Tunnelling was the most hazardous work of all. When working through soft material, there was the danger of collapse and flooding; if the tunnel was being blasted through rock, rock-falls threatened to crush the tunnellers. In both cases, the men had to work long shifts in near-darkness, breathing foul air (made much worse if gunpowder was being used), and usually wet through, thanks to the muddy water that would stream down the walls and collect on the rough floor of the tunnel. Of course, if a good contractor was in charge of the work, injuries and deaths would be minimised. But the number of fatalities and injuries that occurred during the building of the first Woodhead tunnel (1839– 45), caused it to become a *cause célèbre*, instigating the famous 1846 Commons Select Committee 'inquir[ing] into the Condition of Labourers employed in the Construction of Railways and other Public Works'. Edwin Chadwick, a public health activist who was instrumental in forcing the parliamentary enquiry, was highly critical of the carelessness of the contractors and railway company on this project, writing that the 'thirty two killed [at Woodhead] out of such a body of labourers, and one hundred and forty wounded, besides the sick, nearly equal the proportionate casualties of a campaign or a severe battle'.

A GOOD DAY'S PAY...

Generally, a navvy could earn two or three times as much as a farm labourer. During the railway mania years, when labour was in short supply, pay could be as high as six shillings a day. (Of course, when

RIGHT
The construction of an embankment at Boxmoor in Hertfordshire on the London & Birmingham Railway, showing the barrow runs.

LEFT
*Navvies at work on
29th August 1867 at
St Pancras station.*

to oversee it. Usually, this principal contractor would divide the line into sections, then sub-contract the building of each section to an agent, who would then sub-contract small parcels of work in his section, such as a cutting, to 'gangers'. The gangers then employed the navvies.

If the work flowed smoothly and kept to schedule, the system worked well. But if a contractor had underestimated the cost of a job, or if it proved to be more difficult than imagined and the work fell behind schedule, the contractor was out of pocket, often to the extent of going bust – and the navvy lost the money he was owed.

TOMMIES AND SHANTIES

The navvies were also open to exploitation under the 'truck' system. When railways were being built in isolated areas – where the work site could be several miles from the nearest shops – contractors set up 'truck' or 'tommy' shops, where the navvies could buy their beer, food and other provisions. In theory, the system made sense. However, contractors often used the truck and tommy shop system as a way of making money from the men: the goods sold were over-priced and of poor quality. Also, some contractors chose to pay their men once a month, and this provided another opportunity to fleece them – most navvies spent their wages soon after they had been paid and then, to

work was short, for example after the panic of 1847–8, wages also fell, as competition for jobs increased.)

Navvies were rarely, if ever, employed or paid by the railway company sponsoring the building of a railway: the company would appoint a contractor (or contractors) either to do the building work or

LEFT
*Ribblehead Viaduct
in North Yorkshire
crosses Batty Moss,
where navvies lived
while they worked
on the Settle &
Carlisle line.*

live, had to go to the contractor for an advance against the next month's money. This was issued in the form of a ticket that could only be used at the contractor's tommy shop, or in local pubs that gave the contractor a share of the profits from their increased sales. As one of the Woodhead tunnel workers said to the 1846 Select Committee, 'They give us great wages, sir, but they take it all from us again'… Some contractors, such as Peto, despised this system and treated their men honestly; others saw the truck system as their main way of making money, underbidding to get contracts in the knowledge that they would make their profit from beer and food sales to the men. If a navvy was cheated of his wages, lost his job, or heard that pay was higher on another railway elsewhere in the country, he would simply gather his belongings and tramp off to the next job. The system made them professional itinerants, used to temporary jobs, and temporary living conditions.

When lines were built in isolated areas, navvies sometimes lived in temporary huts, called 'shanties'. From newspaper reports these soon achieved notoriety both on account of the squalid accommodation they afforded the occupants, and because of the 'immorality' they encouraged. Shanties could be made of wood, stone, or even mud and turf. Some huts could accommodate more than 100 men and women – navvies would share bunks and it was not uncommon to find a navvy, his wife and young children all sleeping together in one bed.

Living itinerant lives in such conditions, it was accepted that a navvy would take a temporary 'wife' to live with for the duration of the contract. It was practices such as this that so scandalised the press, the clergy and observers, such as Mrs Elizabeth Garnett, at the time. A great legend has built up around the shanty towns and what went on in them. But as the *Oxford Companion to British Railway History* notes, '[they] were a comparatively rare feature of railway building… According to the census returns, railway workers usually lived with the resident population' of the areas they were working in. That said, reports of conditions at Woodhead, and of what went on at Batty Green near Ribblehead Viaduct on the Settle & Carlisle line, show that in some cases, legend was based on fact.

END OF AN ERA

By the 1880s, the great age of the navvy was effectively over in Britain. The Settle & Carlisle, the last major railway to be built using muscle, pick and shovel, had been completed in 1875. Britain's last main-line construction project, the Great Central, remained to be built in the 1890s, but this would be done with the help of steam shovels, each of which did the work of 100 men.

There was still work to be had – some 6,700 miles of railway were constructed between 1870 and 1913, but much of this consisted of local, suburban and cross-country lines. Many navvies chose to take their skills abroad. Brassey had taken his own navvies with him to work on the Pari–Le Havre line in the 1840s and by the latter part of the century navvies from Britain were at work in South and Central America, Australia and Africa, having built key railways in Canada and Europe in the meantime.

A traveller journeying though Argentina by train today, for example, would most likely be on a line built by British navvies: derided in the popular imagination of their day, this robust and remarkable band of men is commemorated in their works not just in Britain, but around the world.

Q AND QI CLASSES

How the British 0-6-0 bowed out, with both a whimper and a bang

Faced with the increased traffic demands of World War II, Bulleid responded with the radically different Q1 class, an 0-6-0 providing maximum power and yet light enough to go almost anywhere on the rail network.

Q Class locomotive No. 30540, fitted by Bulleid with Lemaître blastpipe and large chimney to improve steaming.

First the whimper: Richard Maunsell's Q class 0–6–0 of 1938 represented a mediocre end to a distinguished career. Four years on, his successor as CME of the SR, Oliver Bulleid, delivered the 'bang': an engine that – like it or not – mirrored its time. This last example of that most traditional of British locomotive types, the six-coupled goods engine, incurred more controversy than the thousands of its predecessors built over the previous 100 years. And this on a railway with the lowest freight volume of the Big Four, and where investment in new goods engines had taken a back seat to the advance of suburban electrification. What caused this change of heart was the realisation that the Southern Railway was about to handle an unprecedented freight tonnage: it would become the final link in the supply route that would liberate occupied Europe. Oliver Bulleid, who saw wartime conditions as a challenge rather than a curse, realised the role called for a new breed of locomotive.

The problem faced by both Maunsell and Bulleid was that much of the SR's track had never been upgraded, and weight restrictions were in place on many lines. Maunsell's solution was to keep to the acceptable norms, even if this compromised performance. In contrast, Bulleid took the approach that, above all, generating the maximum power was what

mattered. That placed the emphasis on the boiler, with the rest of the locomotive tailored to it. If that meant dispensing with the nicities, so be it, not that Bulleid needed any excuses to be innovative.

Elsewhere, although many hundreds of six-coupled engines remained in daily use, new design had ended in 1930. That year, Charles Collett filled a gap in the GWR's fleet for a lightweight branch-line goods locomotive with his 2251 Class. The Midland/LMS 0–6–0 had reached its final form with the Fowler 4F of 1924, although construction continued for a further 17 years. On the LNER, the type had reached its pinnacle with Nigel Gresley's powerful J39 of 1926, the finest of these later 0–6–0 designs. During this period, Maunsell had devoted his limited resources to modernising the SR's stock of express passenger and mixed-traffic engines. The freight ranks were enhanced only by a modified version of Robert Urie's S15 4–6–0, an LSWR design dating from 1920, and by a class of 25 goods tank engines, the W 2–6–4T. Consequently, goods traffic remained largely entrusted to pre-grouping 0–6–0s, some – such as the SECR's C class – still very capable but others approaching, or even beyond, retirement date. It was in order to replace at least some of these veterans that, in March 1936, the SR board authorised the building of 20 new 0–6–0s, the Q class.

A SAFE OPTION

Whatever ideas Maunsell and his staff may have had, approval was not accompanied by any incentive to innovate. Simplicity and economy were the guiding factors, along with the requirement to stay within the Civil Engineer's weight restrictions. Wherever feasible, the newcomer employed existing patterns and tooling. For example, the superheated boiler was a smaller version of that successfully employed on the L1 4–4–0 of 1926, slightly tapered and equipped with a Belpaire firebox. Other aspects of the design, such as the long-travel piston valves, drew upon the proven N Class 2–6–0 that Maunsell introduced during his time at the SECR. There were, though, two unusual features: the 21-element Sinuflo superheater, previously used solely on one of the Lord Nelsons, No. 857 *Lord Howe*, and steam-operated reversers of a type that originated with James Stirling, a former Locomotive Superintendent of the South Eastern Railways.

It was during shunting, in which the Q would be engaged frequently, that this device came into its own. It was operated from the footplate by two levers. The first was pushed to select forwards or backwards movement; the second travelled from the horizontal to the vertical and, when pulled to its upright position, allowed steam to enter a piston enclosed in a cylinder placed on the left-hand side of the locomotive, adjacent to the middle wheel splasher. This pushed the valve gear into either forwards or reverse positions, depending on which had been selected by the first lever. The travel of the valve gear stopped immediately the second lever was returned to the horizontal.

A second cylinder, in line with the first, then held the gear in place. The whole device was surprisingly quick-acting – it took only a few seconds to go from full forward to full reverse – which meant that any delay in closing the steam valve could take the engine from forward to reverse gear with the regulator open! However, once the technique was mastered, the benefits of the Stirling reverser could be enjoyed. It was much quicker to operate than the wheel or lever type and, if shuffling to-and-fro in a goods yard, much less fatiguing.

The crew also benefited from a spacious, side-window cab, this despite the restricted width over the sides of 7 ft 9 1/8 in, necessary to meet the SR's gauge constraints. Maximum axleloading was 18 tons, with the rear coupled wheels carrying only 13 tons 10 cwt. Two inside cylinders drove on to a solid crank axle, and Stephenson's link motion was employed.

Steam sanders were placed before the leading coupled wheels and behind the driving wheelset. However, behind the trailing wheels, there was a de-sander or rail washer from which a jet of water issued to wash the sand off the rails when running forward. This was to ensure the working of track circuits was not impaired by sand remaining on the rails. Steam heating connections and vacuum brakes were fitted, usefully extending the engines' scope to passenger trains.

PEDESTRIAN PROGRESS

Costing an inexpensive £7,200 each, the first 11 Q Class 0–6–0s, Nos. 530–40, were outshopped from Eastleigh during 1938. Simultaneously, the works built a quantity of 4,000-gallon tenders, but these were paired with existing U Class 2–6–0s. The Qs had to make do with the superfluous older tenders, these holding 3,500 gallons of water and 5 tons of coal and weighing 40 tons 10 cwt. By the time the first Q 0–6–0 took up duties at Guildford shed, Maunsell had retired to be replaced by Oliver Bulleid, who had been assistant to Gresley on the LNER. Bulleid made it plain that, had he taken charge earlier, these 'pedestrian' (his description) engines would likely have been cancelled, but matters were too far advanced for that. Instead, he had to allow a further nine, Nos. 541–9, to be delivered during 1939.

LEFT
BR Q Class No. 30539 at Brockenhurst in the New Forest, July 1957, with a passenger train for Ringwood.

Bulleid's criticism of the design was not intended as a slight on his predecessor, more a comment on the constraints within which Maunsell had to work. However, it was inescapable that the Q was a poor steamer, something that both Bulleid and, later, BR tried to rectify. Bulleid's method was to enhance the draughting with the fitting of the French-designed Lemâitre multiple-jet blastpipe, a device he also installed in certain of Maunsell's Schools and Lord Nelson locomotives; these engines were easily identifiable from their large diameter and ill-proportioned chimneys.

Although this modification had some effect, a greater improvement resulted from trials conducted at Swindon in 1955 under the acknowledged expert in the field, Sam Ell. The Lemâitre assembly on No. 30549 was replaced by a single blastpipe – its dimensions based on the test findings – with, initially, an ugly stovepipe chimney. However, this was soon exchanged for a similar chimney casting to that used on the Standard Class 4s. The transformation was welcome, as corrosion had made the Lemâitre devices costly to maintain, but there was no rush to implement it: only seven were modified, five during October and November 1961, one year before withdrawals began.

The first of the Qs to be withdrawn was No. 30540, in November 1962. In May 1965, having been relegated to standby and – as in the case of Eastleigh's No. 30548 – snowplough duties, the class was officially dispatched with the retirement of No. 30545 from Nine Elms in London (but not before it had put in some memorable railtour appearances). The 20 Qs ended their days at a variety of depots on the Central and Western Divisions – Bournemouth, Eastleigh, Guildford, Horsham, Nine Elms, Redhill and Three Bridges – with just a single example stationed west of Basingstoke: Salisbury's No. 30531, withdrawn in July 1964.

LIKE CLOCKWORK

The indignity of ugly chimneys, endured by some members of the Q Class, was as nothing compared with the opprobrium heaped upon Bulleid's Q1 0–6–0. When shown a photograph, the LMS's motive power chief, William Stanier, likening what he saw to a clockwork tinplate toy, apparently asked, 'Where do you put the key?' At least one commentator described it as the ugliest locomotive ever built. However, that was missing the point. As with the War Department 2–8–0s and 2–10–0s delivered around the same time, appearance was not a consideration. Undeniably, though, the Q1 took the description 'austerity' to a new level.

In August 1940, the SR's board accepted Bulleid's proposal to build 40 powerful freight locomotives. Starting more or less from scratch, the project would occupy almost two years. Bulleid's radical approach to the design was dictated by circumstances; he knew that much of the SR's system would be off-limits to a modern, conventional heavy freight locomotive, such as the LMS 8F 2–8–0. The Civil Engineer had confirmed to him that an engine with a working weight of under 54 tons (coupled to a tender that did not exceed 39½ tons) would be allowed over 93% of the Southern's route mileage, assuming it also met loading-gauge restrictions.

Moreover, wartime was bringing materials shortages, one of the reasons why the War Department was forced to turn to something simpler and cheaper than the LMS 8F for its purposes. These factors forced Bulleid into a radical re-thinking of the basics of locomotive design, but not one where any experiment was permissible. Therefore, much of the Q1 was straightforward, using existing patterns for many of the components. The cylinder dimensions and Stephenson valve gear, with a maximum valve travel of 6⅞ in, were adapted more or less unchanged from the Q Class.

While the six-coupled wheel arrangement could not have been more quintessentially British, the wheels themselves represented something new. They were of the lightweight double-disc 'Boxpok' pattern first used on the Merchant Navy Pacific of 1941, and, although the inspiration was American, developed by Bulleid in conjunction with the Sheffield steelmakers Firth Brown (hence their description as 'BFB' wheels). They came in around 10% lighter than their spoked equivalents, and Bulleid knew that every such saving would allow him to concentrate weight where it counted: in the power source, the boiler and firebox that would make this the most powerful 0–6–0 ever to run in Britain.

The Q1 mustered over 30,000 lb in tractive effort but weighed only 51 tons 5 cwt, around 14 tons lighter than other classes of comparable weight and power. With the boiler weighing 21¼ tons, the specified weight limit left a maximum of 32¾ tons for the remainder. Further weight savings came from dispensing with traditional embellishments such as running plates alongside the boiler and wheel splashers. Throughout, to save cost as well as weight, fabrications were used instead of castings.

However, it was the boiler, or at least its external appearance, that caused most comment. Bulleid employed a type of lightweight fibreglass, known as Idaglass, for the lagging but, since this could not bear any weight, the boiler cladding was draped over it (rather than wrapped around) and carried on the frames. For convenience, the cladding was in two sections and the underside of the smokebox made flat so that it rested comfortably on the frame and cylinder casting. The boiler barrel itself was in one piece, tapering from 5 ft 9 in diameter to 5 ft, with the firebox backplates and throatplates fabricated using the same flanging blocks as the Lord Nelson 4–6–0s. At 27 sq ft, the area of the firegrate was larger than that of any other British 0–6–0. The smokebox, shaped to give a greater volume than would have been obtained from the equivalent circular variety, contained a five-nozzle multiple jet blastpipe that led to a brutally plain 'bucket' chimney.

One advantage of the Q1's shape was that, like the Merchant Navy, the engine could be superficially cleaned by passing through a carriage washing plant. Fuel was carried in a tender of mainly welded construction, styled like that of the Merchant Navy, carrying five tons of coal and 3,700 gallons of water. It weighed 38 tons, with the coal space designed to be self-trimming to ease the fireman's task.

BARE ESSENTIALS

It is difficult now to appreciate the shock that must have been felt when, on 6th May, 1942, the first of the Q1s appeared at Charing Cross for inspection by the SR's directors. Reflecting Bulleid's predilection for the Continental identification system, which identified the number of coupled axles by letter rather than number, it carried the number C1 (the C standing for three axles). Both the number and the word 'SOUTHERN' on the tender were in sunshine yellow, shaded green, which certainly stood out against the overall plain black livery. Soon No. C1 was demonstrating its capabilities on test freights between Norwood and Chichester. Three months later it was joined by classmate No. C3 in comparative trials with S15 4–6–0 No. 842 hauling 65-wagon trains between Woking and Basingstoke. On one occasion, No. C1 comfortably covered the 24 miles with a mixed train of around 1,000 tons in 58 minutes; the schedule for an 800-ton load was 66 minutes.

Construction of the 40-strong class was divided between the workshops at Brighton (Nos. C1–16, C37–40) and Ashford, Kent (C17–36), with all being delivered during 1942. Unquestionably, the Q1 was a remarkable feat of design and engineering, and compared favourably

LEFT
A typical Q1 duty, albeit on the Bluebell Railway in preservation. Southern freight was mainly sundries, perishables and merchandise, as opposed to mineral traffic.

The boiler was pressed to 230 psi and the firebox design was a shortened form of the Lord Nelson design, and the same flanging and press blocks were used. The boiler was lagged with Idaglass and the casing supported from the frame, enabling the use of light steel-plate cladding.

The Q1 could work over 93% of the Southern network. It weighed 2¼ tons more than the Maunsell Q, but was significantly more powerful, despite its appearance causing adverse comment.

The tender held 5 tons of coal and 3,700 gallons of water. Due to the reduction in material use and weight, some distortion of tender-tank plates was experienced, causing leakage. Although the control layout expedited tender-first running, the tender hindered rearward visibility.

The grate area of 27 sq ft was 30% larger than the Q and provided excellent steaming. Crews were disconcerted by the lack of a running plate to save weight and materials.

A five-jet exhaust stand assisted steaming, and welded fabricated components were used wherever possible to save weight and materials. Any unnecessary fittings were deleted.

TECHNICAL SPECIFICATION

Q and Q1 Classes

	Q class 0-6-0	Q1 class 0-6-0
Cylinders (x2):	19 in x 26 in	19 in x 26 in
(Diameter x Stroke)		
Motion:	Stephenson link motion	
Piston Valves:	10 in	10 in
Boiler Max Dia.	5 ft 0 in	5 ft 9 in
Pressure:	200 psi	230 psi
Heating Surface:	1,247 sq ft	1,472 sq ft
Firebox:	122 sq ft	170 sq ft
Tubes and Flues:	1,125 sq ft	1,472 sq ft
Superheater:	185 sq ft	218 sq ft
Grate Area:	21.9 sq ft	27 sq ft
Wheels: Coupled:	5 ft 1 in	5 ft 1 in
Tender:	4 ft 0 in	3 ft 7 in
Tractive Effort:	26,157 lb	30,080 lb
(@ 85% boiler		
pressure)		
Engine Wheelbase:	16 ft 6 in	16 ft 6 in
Total Wheelbase:	38 ft 11 1/2 in	40 ft 7 1/2 in
Engine Weight:	49 tons 10 cwt	51 tons 5 cwt
Max. Axle Load:	18 tons 0 cwt	18 tons 5 cwt

Bulleid Firth Brown pattern wheels of 5 ft 1 in diameter were used to save weight. The 19-in x 26-in cylinders gave a top speed into the 70-mph range, although officially limited to 55 mph. With 30,000 lb tractive effort, the Q1 was Britain's last and most powerful 0–6–0, capable of hauling a 900-ton train with ease.

with the WD 2–8–0 and 2–10–0, both for cost and performance. There was, though, a price to pay for the 'bare essentials' approach that had delivered its remarkable power-to-weight ratio.

With no protective running plates or splashers, at speed in the rain, fireman and driver leant out of the cab only when necessary! Ladders were needed to reach such items as the washout plugs and clack valves, and for cleaning. However, the omission of steps and rails at the front end was clearly an economy too far, as it made smokebox clearance hazardous. Soon, grab rails were bolted to the smokebox doors and either side of them.

The provision of steam heating enabled the Q1s to haul empty coaching stock, but subsequently found greater use as the engines were increasingly rostered for passenger trains. Crews liked the ease with

which the Q1 could be worked, the relative comfort of the cab and the accessibility of all the key components for maintenance. They were pleasantly surprised to find that, while officially limited to 55 mph, Bulleid's 0–6–0 was capable of up to 75 mph, even running tender-first, although there was a tendency to 'roll' at high speed.

AROUND LONDON

Bulleid intended the engines to have a limited lifespan, but the class remained intact for 21 years and was widely used by both the Southern and British Railways. Their haulage capacity was curbed only by a limited braking capability when hauling loose-coupled, non-vacuum-braked freights. It was this constraint that probably discouraged the Southern from enlarging the class.

In the main, the Q1s were confined to the SR's Western and Central sections, although for a time, some were allocated to Tonbridge in Kent. Examples were based at Eastleigh in Hampshire, Three Bridges in Sussex and at Hither Green in south-east London, but the largest contingents were to be found at Guildford, in Surrey, and at Feltham in south-west London. The depot there served a large marshalling yard and its stud of Q1 0–6–0s spent much of the time on cross-town inter-regional freights. The Q1s could be seen heading prodigious loads to and from Acton, Willesden and Cricklewood, and the Eastern Region yard at Temple Mills, near Stratford. They became a regular sight on the North London line, where their extraordinary appearance was in striking contrast to the traditional LMS and LNER six-coupled goods engines.

The Q1s were also frequently employed on passenger services where they displayed a fair turn of speed, so much so that some believed the Southern would have been better off building more Q1s than adding to the ranks of Battle of Britain and West Country Pacifics (the tractive efforts were comparable).

During the 1960s, home to all 40 Q1s was one of four depots: Eastleigh, Feltham, Guildford or Three Bridges. The first to be withdrawn was No. 33028 in February 1963. It had a defective cylinder that was judged not worth repairing. The final trio consisting of Nos. 33006, 20 and 27 was retired from Guildford in January 1966. Between those dates, Q1s turned up on all manner of specials, including one that took No. 33006, double-heading with U class Mogul No. 31639, from Paddington to Leamington Spa, Stratford-upon-Avon and Wellingborough. On 4th October 1964 the

Locomotive Club of Great Britain's 'Vectis Railtour' included No. 33026 working an eight-coach train between Waterloo and Guildford. It was loaded to 285 tons and topped 50 mph, with a maximum of 56 at Egham.

The doyen of the class, No. C1(33001), was selected to join the National Collection, and went on long-term loan to the Bluebell Railway for many years. The 25-mph speed restriction there precluded drivers confirming the verdict of one SR engineman who, while considering the Q1s good engines, added that, once up to 50 or 60 mph, 'They didn't half rock and roll'. One lasting consequence of the Q1's strange appearance was the response of the 'spotters': seldom can one class of locomotive have had so many nicknames. They were variously known as 'Biscuit Tins', 'Biscuit Barrels', 'Charlies', 'Clockworks', 'Coffee Pots', 'Austerities' and, predictably, 'Ugly Ducklings'. Derogatory names aside, no one could deny that Bulleid's Q1s brought the 108-year history of the British 0–6–0 to a memorable and unendingly controversial conclusion.

covered 459,057 miles (most Q1s had final mileages between 400,000 and 500,000), No. 33001 had already been selected for preservation and been stored at Nine Elms for five months. With the National Collection seeking a permanent home, it joined a number of other famous engines in, first, the paint shop at Stratford Works and then the former Pullman Company works at Preston Park outside Brighton.

On 15th May 1977, No. 33001 went on long-term loan to the Bluebell Railway where it received an 'intermediate' overhaul during 1980 and ran regularly until September 1983. A major overhaul was completed in 1992 and the Q1 – in the original guise as No. C1 – was recommissioned at Sheffield Park on 8th September. Now requiring a further 10-year refit, No. C1 has been relocated to the National Railway Museum, York.

FIRST AND LAST

Unveiled at Brighton Works in March 1942, and after being shown to the Southern's hierarchy six weeks later, the first of the Q1s underwent trials before taking up the kind of duties that would occupy it for the ensuing two decades. Renumbered 33001 by BR in November 1950, it underwent her last general overhaul between 19th January and 14th February 1955 at Ashford Works. By June 1959, No. 33001 was on the books of Tonbridge shed, in Kent, but in February 1961, it was back on the Western Section at Feltham. A move to Guildford came in September 1963.

By the time of its official withdrawal in May 1964, having

LEFT
SR Austerity Class Q1 0–6–0 No. C1, built 1942.

THE ROUTE OF THE THANET BELLE

The first links between London and Kent

In the 19th century, Kent became a battleground for competing rail companies as the SER and LCDR sought to establish lucrative routes to Dover and the coastal towns.

An SECR 4–4–0 awaits departure from the former LCDR terminus at Ramsgate Harbour in pre-grouping years.

During the Napoleonic Wars (1793–1815), the development of the historical and strategically important Medway towns of Chatham, Gillingham, Rochester and Strood was significantly accelerated, creating an urgent requirement for better transport, supply and communication routes with London. The narrow and unmade roads of those days were far from adequate, and thus the most practical form of transport was by coastal cutters and sailing barges between the Thames and Medway ports, but such journeys were vulnerable to enemy action and foul weather. However, as early as 1778, an inland canal had been proposed as a safe route for military traffic between the dockyards of Woolwich and Chatham, and work started on this project in 1800.

The Thames & Medway Canal was surveyed to take a short route cutting across the Hoo Peninsula, and by 1801, the section had been completed from the Thames at Gravesend to a midway point at Higham; the next section from Higham to the Medway required substantial engineering work, including a tunnel through the chalk hills, and was not completed until 1824. The tunnel was a masterpiece of engineering being over 26 ft 6 in wide and 3,931 yd (2½ miles) long and, at the time, it was Britain's second longest tunnel. Notwithstanding the magnificence of its engineering, the tunnel made the canal difficult to navigate by its intended users with their 60-ton sailing barges. Several improvements were made, including the excavation of a cutting – which effectively created two separate tunnels and allowed barges to pass midway – and the provision of a steam launch to carry passengers. However, the enterprise was a commercial failure and, with the growth of railways elsewhere in the country, the canal company decided to build a railway along its route.

The Gravesend & Rochester Railway & Canal Company, as it became, ran beside the canal and through the tunnels where, initially, the track was supported partially on the towing path and partially suspended on wooden piles over the water! Nevertheless, the railway was so successful that, by 1847, canal traffic had all but ceased, and the tunnels had been drained to make way for double track. In the previous year, the line and canal had been acquired by the SER to provide a direct line between London and the Medway towns as part of its expansive development of routes in Kent. The SER had already extended from the early London & Greenwich Railway (1836) through Redhill, Tonbridge, Maidstone and Ashford (1842) to Folkestone (1843) and Dover (1844) and, by the mid-18th century, also had a main line from Ashford to Canterbury and the Thanet coast towns of Ramsgate, Sandwich and Deal. However, the company's route to Thanet and Dover via Redhill was something of a long way round (the route to Dover being at least 20 miles longer than the turnpike route used by stagecoaches), so when the East Kent Railway opened its line from Strood to Chatham, and then to Faversham in 1858, it clearly signalled its ambition of providing a shorter route to Dover.

In 1859, the East Kent Railway revealed its true colours by changing its name to the London Chatham & Dover Railway, and extending through to Canterbury and then Dover (Priory) in 1861. More significantly, the LCDR had also developed an independent route from Strood to London (Victoria) via St Mary Cray, Bromley and Beckenham Junction.

A DICKENS OF A DO

At first, the SER was ill-prepared for competition; it did not enjoy the best of reputations among railway companies and had relished in its virtual monopoly for far too long. In 1865, there was an accident near Staplehurst; men were repairing the line and removed a section of track on a bridge when a boat express from Folkestone approached. The train

LEFT
*The London–
Greenwich Railway.
Elevated on arches
or embankment
along most of its
length, the line
winds through
south-east London.*

was derailed and some of the vehicles ended up in the river; 10 passengers were killed and several injured. As reported before, one of the survivors of the Staplehurst accident was Charles Dickens, whose subsequent account did little to promote the popularity of the much-maligned SER.

Other contemporary writers criticised the railway's uncomfortable track and rolling stock, as well as the high fares being charged on the longer routes to Dover and Folkestone. In contrast, the LCDR's direct line to Dover was an instant commercial success. The new company had also extended from Faversham through Whitstable to Margate and Ramsgate, where it also competed with a much longer SER route from London.

Although much smaller than the SER, the LCDR established an excellent reputation, and was soon running mail trains on its London–Dover services and operating cross-Channel steamers. Stimulated by the competition, the SER invested heavily in expansion and competed fiercely with the LCDR throughout the latter part of the 19th century. The main focus of this competition was for the profitable cross-Channel trade and its associated boat trains; the SER had bought Folkestone Harbour, and its steamers plied between there and Boulogne, whereas the LCDR steamers served the rival Dover to Calais crossing. In 1882, the LCDR stepped up the pace by launching its 'Dover Continental Pullman Car Boat Express' with Pullman coaches borrowed from the LBSC; this train ran between London and Dover and was the forerunner of the 'Golden Arrow' service introduced almost half a century later. Although the rivalry had provided an initial stimulus for development, as the 19th century drew to a close, both companies were becoming battle-weary from a long period of largely destructive and unnecessary competition, during which they had pursued custom with rival branch lines and services.

HIGHAM TUNNEL
AS IT EXISTED BEFORE THE CONSTRUCTIO
OF THE NORTH KENT RAILWAY.

The fierceness of the competition, which left a legacy of unreasonably duplicated stations and services in many parts of Kent, has often been blamed on the personalities that chaired the undertakings. On the SER, Edward Watkin – with his proud vision of connecting England's industrial heartland with continental Europe via the railways under his influence and a tunnel under the Channel – was well-known for his pugnacity, whilst James Staats Forbes, chairman of the LCDR, had steadfastly refused to give in to SER pressure, and had invested recklessly in competing with his rival at every opportunity.

Eventually, after Watkin's retirement from the SER and with the LCDR on the verge of insolvency, it was agreed that it would be best if the two railways could work together. With Parliamentary approval, the two companies (although retaining their separate legal identities) were operated as one under a jointly appointed management committee, known as the South Eastern & Chatham Railway from 1st January 1899.

The SECR was well represented with its London termini; together with the London Brighton & South Coast Railway, the LCDR had shared the terminus at Victoria, while the SER had its original terminus at London Bridge (a location also shared with the LBSC), together with the prestigious stations at Charing Cross (opened in 1864) and Cannon Street (1866).

THE FOUR "BELLES" RING THE
SOUTHERN COAST
DEVON BELLE
OBSERVATION CAR
THANET BELLE
NEW TRAIN
LONDON
BOURNEMOUTH BELLE
BRIGHTON BELLE
ALL PULLMAN
COMFORT
Ask for details
at Stations

Under the joint management committee, the SECR concentrated all boat trains and the most important express services at Victoria, whilst the other termini mainly handled the intensive services of commuter, local and stopping trains. There were also healthy freight operations with excellent traffic flows serving the naval dockyard at Chatham, the Kent coalfield and the channel ports.

RADICAL CHANGES

The SECR's Locomotive, Carriage & Wagon Department was established at Ashford Works, with Harry Wainwright from the SER in charge and a former LCDR man, Robert Surtees, as his deputy. They produced an outstanding range of locomotives, including the elegant D and E Class express passenger 4–4–0s, known affectionately as 'coppertops', all turned out in the most attractive new livery of ornately lined Deep Brunswick Green.

Passenger rolling stock was also gradually improved and was generally finished in the deep crimson livery that had been used by the SER. In 1913, the gifted Irish engineer Richard Maunsell (pronounced 'Mansell'), who had trained under Henry Ivatt at the Great Southern & Western Railway's Inchicore Works in Dublin, took over as CME and continued to improve the efficiency and quality of the SECR's locomotives and rolling stock; this helped enormously in burying the poor reputation that trains in Kent had endured during the competitive years.

World War I had an enormous impact on the SECR, primarily because, geographically, it was the closest British railway to the conflict. Huge quantities of troops and supplies were shipped to the Channel ports, which stretched the railway's resources to the limit; austerity measures were imposed, stations closed (some of which were never to reopen) and the elegant pre-war liveries gave way to 'austerity grey' for locomotives and dull brown for passenger stock.

LEFT
The Thanet Belle *provided a luxury service between the Isle of Thanet and the capital for wealthier holiday-makers on summer Saturdays.*

ABOVE

The aftermath of the accident at Staplehurst in Kent, June 1865.

After the war, despite severe financial constraints, the SECR made a tremendous effort to rebuild its services; the prestigious *Thanet Pullman Limited*, the first all-Pullman express to run in Kent, was introduced in July 1921, running on Sundays only non-stop from Victoria to Margate, which was later extended to Broadstairs and Ramsgate. In another initiative to rebuild the local economy, Maunsell worked with the Government to produce locomotive components at Woolwich Arsenal, which provided employment for the men that had previously been involved in making war materials.

With the grouping of 1923, the SECR became the Eastern Division of the SR, and many senior posts in the new organisation were filled by SECR stalwarts, including Maunsell, who became the Southern's Chief Mechanical Engineer. Naturally, the SR continued to develop its services in Kent, especially the boat trains and cross-channel steamers, but the Thanet route to the resorts of the Margate, Ramsgate and Broadstairs also received ls. attention, not least because of their heavy summer excursion traffic.

After nationalisation, the former SECR lines in Kent became part of the Southern Region of BR and, thanks to the excellent husbandry of Maunsell at Ashford Works, many veteran 0–6–0s and 4–4–0s continued to work the Medway and Thanet services until the end of steam. In May 1948, BR introduced a new all-Pullman train, the *Thanet Belle*, which ran on summer Saturdays from Victoria via Chatham to Ramsgate; it was all in the spirit of the Pullman services pioneered years before by the LCDR and SECR.

In 1951, the schedule was amended and three coaches were detached at Faversham for Canterbury; the train was re-branded the *Kentish Belle*, but the Canterbury coaches were not popular and were discontinued the following year. Nevertheless, the *Kentish Belle* presented a magnificent spectacle, running high-speed between Victoria and Ramsgate, usually with 10 Pullman coaches in the charge of a Bulleid Pacific; the service continued to the end of the 1958 summer season when the route was electrified.

HOP-PICKERS SPECIALS

Hops are a key ingredient in the brewing of beers, and during the September harvest, it had become common practice to recruit casual labour from poor areas, such as the slums of London's East End. As many as 80,000 men, women and whole families would migrate to the hop fields of Kent for what many regarded as a paid 'summer holiday', living in crude tents, shelters or 'hopper's huts' set up in the fields. The SER and its successors laid on hundreds of special trains from London Bridge and other stations to carry them; the crowded trains were composed of old coaches with very basic accommodation, retained specially for these services, and were often hauled by equally old locomotives, pressed into service for the occasion. The hop-pickers enjoyed plenty of beer, and there was a great deal of merriment, with festivals and fairs to celebrate the end of the harvest before they returned home; under the circumstances, it is probably just as well that the railway kept its oldest coaches for this traffic.

NINE ELMS SHED

The evolution of London's major locomotive repair facility

From its origins as the London & Southampton Railway's London depot, the Nine Elms Shed underwent multiple renovations throughout its long history, evolving into a major site for locomotive manufacturing and repair.

What was the Southern's largest locomotive shed is now buried under the site of London's relocated (now New) Covent Garden Market relocated yet again in 2017 to make way for the development of 100,000 new homes on the old site. In its heyday, Nine Elms stabled more than 200 engines in a sprawling complex, which was rebuilt as traffic on the LSWR grew; the company workshops were also located next door, until their move to Eastleigh. As electrification grew on the SR, Nine Elms diminished, but it remained a stronghold for steam until the end, although the dirt, grime and decay apparent in the 1960s was a far cry from its halcyon days before 1939.

When the London & Southampton Railway opened in 1838, its first terminal station in the capital was situated at Nine Elms. Before the arrival of the railway, the area was described by one contemporary writer as 'a low swampy district, occasionally overflowed by the Thames'. It was supposedly named in the 17th century for a series of elm trees close by, and the combination of the low-lying ground, willow beds and windmills led some to attribute something of a Dutch character to the neighbourhood. Unfortunately, this sylvan scene was soon to be changed for ever, as timber yards, lime kilns, breweries and many other industrial concerns were established in the area.

The new London & Southampton terminus was designed by William Tite. An early company report noted that there had been 'no unnecessary expense in architectural designs or decorations', and the original Nine Elms locomotive depot was built close to this station, near the Vauxhall end of Nine Elms Lane.

The London & Southampton became the London & South Western Railway in 1839, the name change being in part a reflection of the fact that it had begun the process of extending its suburban and main-line network into the south and south west of England. However, the Nine Elms terminus soon proved to be too remote from the centre of London, and a 1½-mile extension,

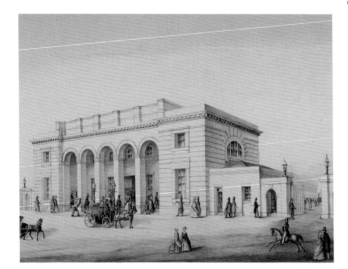

carried on 290 arches, was built to a new station at Waterloo which opened in 1848.

The consequence of this major development was the closure of Nine Elms, and in time, the reconstruction of the locomotive depot. The original shed was demolished and its site covered by new widened running lines from Waterloo. The facilities provided for LSWR locomotives consisted of a seven-road through shed with a 40-ft turntable at either end; in addition, two coal stages were also provided. This depot, opened in 1865, survived for almost 20 years before being replaced by a larger loco shed in 1876.

EXPANSION

The old structure was superseded by a massive roundhouse, built at right angles to the main line. This roundhouse had 26 separate locomotive roads, radiating from two 42-ft turntables. To service the large number of locomotives stabled at the shed, a new double-sided coal stage was also built.

In parallel with this work, the company also continued to develop its own railway works at Nine Elms. A facility had first opened in 1839, and the first engine had been built on the site in 1844. Further expansion took place in 1855 with the purchase of a further 30 acres of land, although in truth, the location chosen was not ideal; by the 1870s, the LSWR works was surrounded on all sides by the river, industry and densely packed residential streets. Over 2,400 men were employed at the works, and at its height, it built around 30 locomotives and carried out a further 400 repair jobs each year.

Despite the extensive facilities provided with the opening of the roundhouses in 1876, this was not the end of expansion at Nine Elms. The introduction of larger main-line passenger engines by the company meant that in 1885, the LSWR completed a further expansion with the building of a large 15-road singleended shed measuring 365 by 265 ft to the west of the roundhouse depot. The new shed was similar in design to others provided by the company at Eastleigh and Salisbury, and was served by another turntable, this time 50 ft in length. In the event, the new shed was clearly not large enough, for it was extended in length within four years. By the turn of the 20th century, Nine Elms shed was the largest on the LSWR and had a locomotive allocation of around 200 engines, used on a variety of services, including express passenger, suburban and goods trains.

TRANSPLANTING ELMS

The aforementioned difficulties in operating a large railway works in the centre of a major city worsened as the 19th century progressed. The 45-acre Nine Elms railway factory became more and more burdensome for the LSWR, and at one stage, locomotive construction had been abandoned altogether. Production did begin again in 1886, but with no possibility of expansion, the company made the fateful decision to move its facilities away from the capital.

Two years earlier in 1884, the LSWR had sought parliamentary powers to purchase land at Eastleigh in Hampshire and in 1891, it made the first move to relocate its workshop operation by moving the Carriage & Wagon department there. This did free up space at Nine Elms, but the final move westwards was inevitable, especially since land there was needed for the LSWR traffic department. In 1898, the company acquired a further 200 acres of land at Eastleigh with the purpose of building a new locomotive works. In the event, although construction of the works and a new engine shed complex began in 1900, it was almost nine years before production finally began properly at Eastleigh. The Nine Elms boiler shop, built as recently as 1893, was taken down and relocated at the new works, and most of the machine tools from the London works were also transported to Hampshire for reuse.

The final locomotive built at Nine Elms, the 832nd to be constructed there, was finally completed in June 1908, and the first to be built at Eastleigh rolled out of the works there in September 1910.

LEFT
The roundhouse at Nine Elms on 11th June 1902.

Following the closure of Nine Elms Works, the LSWR took the opportunity to remodel the track there, allowing the widening of the metropolitan extension viaduct and the addition of more running lines, some to accommodate the onset of suburban electrification. Parts of the old works were also converted for use by the goods department, with the old erecting shop being rebuilt as an empties shed, and locomotive department offices occupied by goods accounts clerks.

'NEW' SHED

The move to Eastleigh also prompted further expansion and changes at Nine Elms shed. The old roundhouse, previously used for suburban tank locomotives following the construction of the 1885 shed, was finally demolished in 1909 as electrification began to displace engines of this type; the 200 locomotives stabled at Nine Elms in 1900 had shrunk to 162 by the time of grouping in 1923. A new mileage yard was eventually built on the site of the roundhouse, and a further 10-road extension was built next to the old 1885 straight shed. Costing £26,000, this structure, capable of housing 60 locomotives, became known to enginemen as the 'New Shed'. The LSWR also took the opportunity to modernise office accommodation, as well as improving stores and repair facilities clearly necessary as a consequence of the works relocation. A final improvement to the enlarged 25-road depot was the provision of a new 65-ft turntable.

LEFT
No. 30320, a Drummond M7 0-4-4T, typical of the Waterloo station pilots provided by Nine Elms after their earlier careers on suburban services.

Following the Great War, when land adjoining the depot was requisitioned and used to grow potatoes for the war effort, the LSWR had little opportunity to invest further at Nine Elms, with one distinctive exception. Construction of the massive 400-ton coaling plant was begun before grouping, but not complete until 1923, by which time the shed had become part of the Southern Railway. Costing over £9,000, the ferro-concrete structure dominated the shed complex and was fitted with a hoist that raised loaded coal wagons to its top, where they were tipped, and dropped coal into the hopper below. The coal could then be fed by gravity into the tenders of engines positioned underneath.

POST-WAR DECLINE

Nine Elms was the largest locomotive depot on the Southern, but with the continued growth of electrification in the 1920s and '30s, there was little further investment in the shed before World War II. A water-softening plant was installed in 1930, and six years later, an engine-washing facility was added. Nine Elms shed suffered during the Blitz of 1940 and '41. Its location meant that it was hit many times by both incendiary and high explosive bombs, with the 'Old' 1885 shed particularly badly affected. Following the end of hostilities and the ensuing austerity, little if any of the damaged roofing was replaced, so that by the 1960s, the 'Old' shed had no roof to speak of and had become no more than an open store for locomotives.

The 200 engines cared for by Nine Elms in its heyday of 1900 had shrunk to less than 100 by the end of the 1950s, a figure that shrunk even more dramatically in the final years of steam. Despite the diminution of status, in the 1950s it could still boast a complement of over 200 drivers and firemen, as well as other trades such as fitters, carpenters, cleaners, turntable operators and office staff. The shed was used to prepare the Bulleid Pacific No. 34051 *Winston Churchill*, normally

stabled at Salisbury, when she hauled the funeral train of Sir Winston Churchill in January 1965.

By 1966, only 24 engines were allocated to Nine Elms, a total that included a number of BR standard locomotives and SR West Country Pacifics. The once-bustling depot was a forlorn sight in the 1960s, with semiderelict buildings and debris strewn around the complex. One railwayman, John Wickham, remembered Nine Elms, saying, 'I never saw such a filthy hole in all my life. It is hardly surprising they shut it down'. Despite the awful conditions, though, staff soldiered on, preparing engines for duty and suffering poor maintenance standards, non-existent cleaning and shortages of such basic tools as firing shovels and oil feeders, which firemen hid to prevent them being stolen.

The sometimes dramatic landscape of the semi-derelict shed proved an ideal location for the artist David Shepherd to sketch and paint. He spent many hours at the depot in the last weeks of its existence, producing one of his most famous paintings, *Nine Elms, the Final Hours*, there. The engines still stabled at the shed were, he argued, 'the grimy workhorses in the twilight of their years, neglected, forlorn, but still working'.

When Nine Elms shed finally closed in 1967, there were still 31 locomotives there, and it was some weeks before they were removed for scrapping. Soon, the whole depot was razed to the ground, to make way for the relocated Covent Garden Market.

RIGHT
'Nine Elms, the Final Hours' by David Shepherd.

GRADIENT AND INCLINE WORKING

Risking life and limb on Britain's steepest grades

Steep ascents and descents were the ultimate test for railway engineers, crew and locomotives alike, pushing men and machines to the limit.

An all-out attack on the foot of the 1 in 100 incline from Little Bowden Crossing to Kelmarsh, as an 8F train engine and banker handle a 1,200-ton train from Toton to Willesden in August 1964.

If there was one railway-operation skill that truly sorted the men from the boys, it was successfully working up- and downhill with handbraked unfitted trains. Controlling descents was a black art, and if the train crew and other operators didn't succeed, other black arts involving hearses could be called into action.

Gradients were always a problem, and early railway engineers strove to minimise them, often at very considerable cost, their reasons being the weakness of early locomotives and their doubt in the ability of adhesion to put the power down on to the rail. Early engineers tended to follow a canal philosophy, often following a sinuous level contoured course, and then achieving a height change by the use of a cable-hauled incline. This could be self-acting where

the loads primarily descended, like the Blorenge Incline on Hill's tramway between Blaenavon and Llanfoist, or use a stationary steam winding engine to haul loads upgrade, as on Robert Stephenson's Stanhope & Tyne or Jessop's Cromford & High Peak railways. In a few cases, waterwheels were used for winding, as on Treffry's Carmears incline on the Cornwall Minerals Railway in the Luxulyan Valley. A superb example of a working water-balance incline can still be seen in action in the Lynton–Lynmouth Cliff Railway opened in 1890, whilst an electrically wound incline can be seen in action on the Bowes Railway. An unusual method of working on the Taff Vale Railway was used at Pwllyrhebog, near Tonypandy, where a double-track cable-worked incline of 1 in 13 for 40 chains connected collieries at Clydach. There was no winding engine, but all trains had locomotives at the downhill end, and the haulage rope was attached directly to them. According to the balance of the two loads, both engines could apply power, the descending train assisting the ascending one with both its weight and the efforts of its engine working hard downhill. Equally, both engines could apply braking power should a coupling or cable fail, and the incline never experienced a fatal accident in its 88 years of operation, despite considerable loads being conveyed. Three special 0–6–0T engines were designed for the incline: they had large 5-ft 3-in driving wheels – to clear the dolly sheaves – sloping crown sheets and a tapered boiler barrel, to ensure that the firebox crown was kept covered when facing downhill.

BREAKAWAYS

Inclined planes required intensive manpower: hangers-on, brakesmen, winding-engine crews, dolly oilers and ropegreasers, as well as inspectors; the last were necessary as a breakaway was almost always disastrous. One only has to look in the catch pit near the foot of the CHPR's Sheep Pasture incline to see the twisted wreckage of wagons that went on a wild run as late as the 1960s. In addition, trains had to be broken up and remarshalled, making inclines an undesirable obstruction to growing rail traffic. Except for exceptional locations, the inclined plane was not really an economic solution to overcoming gradients. Railway operators and engineers therefore began to seek alternatives; one of the first was devised by Matthew Murray in Leeds in June 1812 to overcome the dismaying grades of the Middleton Colliery Railway. He added a rack alongside one running rail and fitted a driven pinion to *Salamanca*, which enabled the locomotive to ascend and descend successfully.

LEFT
The Lynton–Lynmouth Cliff Railway is still powered entirely by water. Filled ballast tanks on the descending car haul the lighter unfilled car uphill by a continuous cable; the process is then reversed, the tank of the ascending car being emptied at the base station.

Standard Class 4 No. 75024 banking a train of Presflo powder wagons on Shap.

Other railway engineers surveyed railways to avoid these difficulties; Brunel's GWR from Paddington so assiduously avoided high ground that it was nicknamed 'The Great Way Round'. However, Joseph Locke had much greater confidence in the increasing puissance of the steam locomotive, and engineered lines with inclines such as Woodhead, Shap, Beattock and Honiton, which, whilst they still restricted the loads that could be hauled, nevertheless enabled the growing traffic demands to be handled.

The increasing power of locomotives led to some being converted to 'normal', if spectacular, haulage; examples include Hopton on the CHPR and the Werneth incline approaching Oldham. Here, the general approach of footplate crews was 'fill her up, wind her up and open right up', in other words, create a deep, hot fire to withstand the ferocity of the blast, ensure that the boiler has plenty of water, then stop adding cold fuel and water, which would reduce steam generation, and charge the foot of the climb at maximum possible speed; then give the engine everything it can use: full main valve, as near maximum cutoff that the cylinders and exhaust blast can stand without choking, and let her rip. Sadly, today, all too few people have witnessed the shattering passage of an engine being worked in this manner, normally accompanied by torrents of incandescent coals and even flames from the chimney, a red hot smokebox and a corrugated barrage of exhaust noise never really equalled by any other form of land transport. Even passengers became aware of a drumming hail of cinders on the carriage roofs as the train triumphantly blasted its way to the summit; however, it was not all hell and no notion. The driver would be intensely attuned to his engine, ever alert with regulator and sands for a slip that, on steep gradients like this, could lead to ignominious defeat, especially on a bad rail, and possibly major mechanical damage to the engine unless skilfully handled. Priming was a further risk, which could shatter a cylinder or hugely reduce performance.

When the summit was attained, the engine was eased, the blower turned on to prevent a blow-back, the injector started to ensure that the boiler-level was restored and the fire replenished and cooled, avoiding a huge waste of steam through the safety valves. This type of ascent, beloved by admirers of steam, was spectacular, and demonstrated the explosively responsive and variable power of steam locomotives, but it was not viewed with much affection by maintenance or financial staff. In addition, whilst there was quite a number of short and sharp

RIGHT
An Austerity 2–8–0 shoves hard on the buffers of the ex-Devon Belle observation car, as a special climbs to Copy Pit summit.

inclines of this nature – for example Exeter Central, leaving Bradford Exchange, Cockett and Dainton – the majority of major climbs was longer, and required a different approach.

In overcoming longer heavy gradients, several techniques could be adopted, the first being the reduction of trainloads to enable the existing engines to handle the worst gradients – commonly known as the ruling gradient – unassisted. The principle was that the locomotive should be able to restart its train unassisted on the line's most difficult banks; beyond that, the fireman's skill and boiler horsepower determined the speeds at which these longer climbs could be surmounted.

The policy adopted by the Midland, which was thought by Cuthbert Hamilton Ellis to belong to a 'Society for the Prevention of Cruelty to Locomotives', was to keep trainloads light and add pilot engines at the slightest sniff of an overload, or before the train tackled arduous stretches of line like Desborough and Sharnbrook banks on the London main line, particularly for up coal trains, and the Settle & Carlisle's passenger services. Its method of using small locomotives like this was a case of being penny-wise and poundfoolish; the resulting congestion of pilot locomotives' movements undoubtedly contributed to the catastrophic Hawes Junction accident in 1910.

The LNWR took exactly the opposite viewpoint; it had larger engines, but thrashed almost all of them to within a hair's breadth of their mechanical lives, relying on the driver's judgement as to the load that he could successfully convey; and if some climbs couldn't be

LEFT
Two 57XX GWR
0–6–0PTs head
and bank a steel
train up Old Hill
Bank, through
Cradley Heath.

managed, a pilot could always be put on in front or a banker at the rear. The latter practice was used by LNWR passenger trains on Shap, initially with the spectacular and ultimately unacceptably percussive technique of the banker chasing the train on to the gradient and buffering up on the move.

Later, banking operations became safer and more disciplined, if less exciting; the train to be assisted would come to a stand at the appropriate starting signal and a banking engine would buffer up to the rear of the train. Normally, unless intermediate stops or down-gradients were to be encountered within the banked section, the banker would not be coupled to the train; an exception was on the Somerset & Dorset where freight bankers from Radstock to Masbury were coupled on, but released by the guard using an extended coupling iron, which was hung and replaced on the banker's smokebox handrail before being dropped off near the summit. A banked train started its journey, given the road, when the rear engine notified the train engine that it was in position by whistling up a double crow (four short blasts, and one long, sounded twice) whistle, to which the train engine responded with a single crow (at many locations the banker would again crow as it commenced pushing, which ensured that it did not lose contact with the train). The train engine then leant into the collar as well, and set off in a vigorous charge at the climb ahead. One other point of operating procedure was that the guard's tail lamp would be removed and replaced by a tail lamp on the banker, enabling signalmen to observe the complete passage of the train and display a red light to the rear.

BANKING EXPERIENCE

As usual, the GWR did things differently; it did not permit the banking of passenger trains in the rear, and insisted that pilot engines being attached to assist were placed inside the train engine, the logic being that this engine driver was the more experienced and senior man and should remain in charge of the train, and that the larger engine, usually with a leading bogie, should head one with a pony truck or no guiding wheels. This system had a major advantage, as the senior man kept control of the brake, and this could prevent first-class rows and even fisticuffs, sometimes involving soupstained dining-car staff.

Despite the difficulties of heavy trains, bad rail conditions and, in later years, poorly maintained engines and execrable-quality coal, heavy passenger and freight trains were worked up and down difficult, steeply graded lines with locomotives whose power, on paper, would today be regarded as risible. In addition, try confronting the driver, controlling 3,300 hp of one of today's continuously braked freights, with the typical task of a steam-freight driver up to 1968. The prospect of negotiating even the Midland main line's moderate but lengthy banks with an engine like an 8F – capable of 1,300 hp, with a load of 1,400 tons and controllable stopping power only from a 20-ton brake van in the rear, a tender brake and a locomotive steam brake – would make many blench, and the crews needed the judgement of Solomon and nerves of steel. Yet steam footplate crews did it daily for over 140 years. It was all down to extraordinary skill, experience and judgement; no wonder they found promotion to passenger links with fully braked trains a sinecure in comparison.

STOP THE TRAIN

The astonishing survival of hand-braked wagons on BR until the 1970s made steep descents risky. Stopping and pinning down handbrakes should have made the train controllable; if it wasn't, a terrifying 'wild run' would ensue, with perhaps over 1,000 tons hurtling out of control. Reversing the engine could help, but loss of adhesion made matters worse, so sands full on and 'jag' breaking was often the best policy, but furious whistling and a clear road ahead was even better.

The Brecon & Merthyr's fearsome 7-mile bank at 1 in 38 down from Torpantau to Talybont on Usk witnessed the horrendous runaway of a triple-engined coal train that was estimated to have attained over 90 mph before jumping the rails, killing all but one of the crew. The construction of a very steep emergency siding halfway down at Pentir Rhiw helped, but steep descents had to be treated with the utmost respect; in their early years, even the biggest diesels had to be coupled to a 40-ton brake tender to stand any chance of controlling even a 4F load.

THE STREAMLINERS
& THE RECORD BREAKERS

—

WORLD WAR II LOOMS

THE STREAMLINERS & THE RECORD BREAKERS

GWR Streamlined Railcar No.1, built by AEC Southall with a Park Royal body, entering service in December 1933.

Manorbier Castle, *showing the rudimentary fairings and Kühler-style bullet nose applied by Collett. The one-piece wheel splasher design was retained by Hawksworth on the post-war 10XX Counties.*

In 1930, German State Railways tested the Schienenzeppelin railcar, which featured a streamlined body shape, and in 1931, it established a new speed record of 143 mph between Berlin and Hamburg. This was followed in 1932 by *Fliegender Hamburger*. This two-car, diesel-electric set made its first experimental run from Berlin to Hamburg in October 1932; two months later, it set a new record by covering the 178 miles between the cities in 138 minutes (reaching up to 100 mph), and was able to maintain these speeds when brought into regular passenger service in May 1933. Streamlining was soon adopted by other continental European and North American railways, frequently for fast, medium-to-long-distance operations. In Britain, though, it made its debut in the somewhat humbler form of a 'trial diesel unit' purchased by the GWR in 1933 for use around west London, Slough and Reading.

The new railcar was a 69-seater whose ultra-economical running costs (quoted as 3 farthings, or threequarters of a pre-decimal penny, per mile) made it a viable alternative to the GWR's ageing fuel-hungry steampowered auto-trains. However, for the journalists who accompanied the vehicle on its test-run between Paddington and Reading on 1st December 1933, its principal points of interest were its unconventional shape, described by *The Locomotive* as 'resembl[ing] a huge seaplane float,' and the freedom from vibration and buffeting afforded by its streamlining. A correspondent for *The Times* noted that 'in the streamlined car the presence of another train... on the adjoining line was not perceptible,' even when travelling at speeds of up to 60 mph. This smooth running was the result of extensive wind-tunnel testing by the unit's London-based creators, Hardy Motors (later AEC Ltd) of Southall and Park Royal Coachworks of Willesden; it delighted the GWR officials on board, who declared the Paddington–Reading trial an outstanding success, put the streamlined vehicle into full-time operation just three days later, and went on to employ many similarly designed diesels for its commuter traffic over the following years.

C B Collett, the Great Western's Chief Mechanical Engineer, had not been involved in the railcar's genesis; but, by late 1934, it was being suggested to him that streamlining, having proved its value on diesels, could also be an effective element in steam locomotive design. He responded, in the words of his biographer, J E Chacksfield, by 'ordering the [GWR] drawing office to prepare some diagrams based on his own application of plasticine to a model of a Castle Class'. During 1935, these moulding-clay-inspired modifications, which included 'aerodynamic' bullet-noses, and reshaped cabs and tenders, were applied to two real-life locos, *Manorbier Castle* and *King Henry VII*. Sadly, the alterations did little for the engines' aesthetic appeal, and, as Chacksfield points out, the

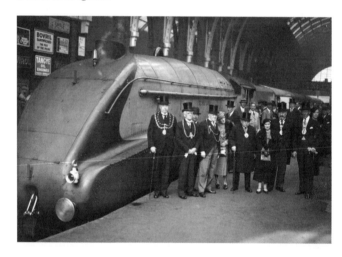

BELOW

A group of dignitaries stands beside Silver Link *at King's Cross on 30th September 1935, including the Lord Mayors of Newcastle, London and Darlington.*

installation of metal 'fairing' (external surrounds) over their cylinders caused the motion bearings to overheat, consequently marring, rather than enhancing, their performance. No further steam-locomotive streamlining ever took place on the GWR, and *Manorbier Castle's* fittings were eventually removed in 1947, although *King Henry VII* retained her contoured cab (though not her other accretions) for the rest of her working life.

SPEED TRIALS

While these unsuccessful experiments were in progress on the GWR, more radical streamlining schemes were taking shape at the London & North Eastern. Its directors were planning a high-speed service between the capital and Newcastle; in March 1935, having considered and rejected the idea of operating this with German-built, *Fliegender Hamburger*-style diesel-electrics (which, as data from their makers revealed, would have been able to manage no more than 63 mph on the LNER's main line), they gave the go-ahead to their CME, Nigel Gresley, to begin developing a state-of-the-art, streamlined A4 Pacific steam locomotive for what would soon be named the 'Silver Jubilee' express.

This was to be the latest addition to a family of Gresley-designed engines that had already proved themselves capable of outstanding turns of speed. On 30th November 1934, an A1 Pacific, *Flying Scotsman*, had, according to dynamometer readings, reached 100 mph (though this was not authenticated by onboard timings) on a run down Stoke Bank, south of Grantham in Lincolnshire. There were no such ambiguities during the trip undertaken, on 5th March 1935, by *Papyrus*, an A3 Class Pacific boasting various improvements over the A1, including higher boiler pressure and tractive effort: on this journey, 100 mph was exceeded for some 12 miles, and a record-breaking maximum of 108 mph attained. However, even these

1935

March – Great Western adds streamlining to the body of a King Class steam loco, *King Henry VII*. Another engine, *Manorbier Castle*, is similarly adapted at about the same time

5th March – LNER A3 Pacific *Papyrus* reaches 108 mph

22nd September – the first streamlined (A4) LNER Pacific (*Silver Link*), completed earlier this month, just exceeds 101 mph on a test run

27th September – *Silver Link* achieves a speed of 112½ mph

30th September – LNER *Silver Jubilee* express, drawn by A4 Pacifics, goes into service between London and Newcastle

1936

11th May – Germany's Borsig locomotive 05.002 sets a new world record for steam traction – 124½ mph

was informed of it by the dynamometer staff'. He had cause for more celebration five days later, when, on another test run, *Silver Link* and its 'Silver Jubilee' carriages twice reached 112½ mph, setting a new British speed record. O S Nock's *Speed Records on Britain's Railways* notes that on this trip, *Silver Link* also shattered two world records for both steam and diesel traction by exceeding 100 mph continuously for 25 miles, and covering 41.2 miles (between Hatfield and Huntingdon) at an average of 100.6 mph.

The four-hour booked time for the LNER's *Silver Jubilee* King's Cross–Newcastle service, launched on 30th September 1935, was easily within the capabilities of the Gresley A4s, as was the six hours scheduled for the journey between London and Edinburgh on another of the company's flagship trains, the *Coronation*. This new Anglo-Scottish service was introduced on 5th July 1937, and it can scarcely have been a coincidence that the LMS chose the same day to inaugurate its own express, the *Coronation Scot*, which would cover the 400-odd miles from Euston to Glasgow in six-and-a-half hours, and be drawn by the LMS's own streamlined engine, *Coronation*.

Like the A4, the Coronation Class (24 of which were eventually built) was partly inspired by European – and, specifically, German – technical developments. The LMS's CME, William Stanier, had the opportunity to see some of these

A4 class 4-6-2 locomotive No. 60017 Silver Fox at King's Cross, about 1960.

achievements would soon be eclipsed by the new A4, whose first example, named *Silver Link*, was completed on 7th September 1935. With a boiler pressure and tractive effort (respectively, 250 psi and 35,455 lb at 85%) substantially greater than the A3s, and a body whose aerodynamic contours not only reduced by more than 130 hp the power needed to operate at 90 mph in windless conditions – and also helped to lift smoke from the exhaust away from the driver's cab, thereby improving visibility – it promised great things, and did not disappoint on its first major outing: a 101 mph-plus descent of Stoke Bank on 22nd September. Gresley was on board the *Silver Link*-headed train that day, and afterwards commented to reporters, 'Here is an engine only a fortnight out of the LNER works at Doncaster. Yet it ran at 100 mph so freely and easily that I did not realise that the speed was so high till I

1937				1938
27th August – LNER's Pacific A4 *Silver Fox* reaches 113 mph	**25th May** – London Midland & Scottish unveils its first streamlined locomotive, *Coronation*, and *Coronation Scot* train at its Crewe works	**29th June** – the *Coronation Scot* train, drawn by *Coronation*, makes a promotional run from London Euston to Crewe and back, attaining a top speed of 112½ mph (114 mph is indicated by the engine's speed recorder)	**5th July** – LMS *Coronation Scot* goes into service between Euston and Glasgow. On the same day, a new LNER express, the *Coronation* (drawn by Pacific A4s) begins operating between London King's Cross and Edinburgh	**3rd July** – LNER A4 Pacific *Mallard* reaches 125 (or perhaps 126 mph) on a test run; either figure represents a still-unbroken world speed record for steam locomotives

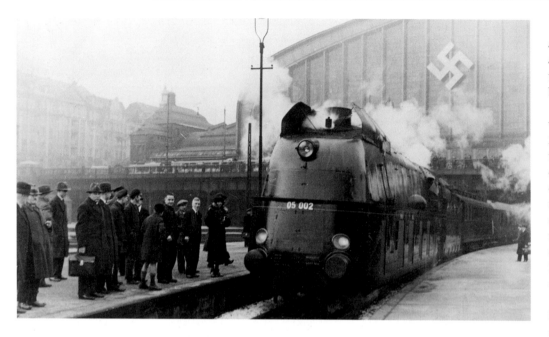

ABOVE

German State Railways Borsig streamlined Pacific 05.002 held the world speed record for steam from 1936 until it was captured by Mallard in 1938.

at first hand during a visit to Germany made during 1936 in his capacity as President of the Institute of Locomotive Engineers. His experiences there left him unconvinced of the benefits of streamlining: J E Chacksfield's *Sir William Stanier: A New Biography* states that he felt its advantages were overrated, and recommended to the LMS board that they should not adopt it. The directors disagreed, insisting that the Coronation Class incorporate aerodynamic contouring. The plans for the new engine class (which, in other respects, was essentially a more powerful version of the company's existing Princess Royal 4–6–2 design) were largely drawn up by its Derby-based Chief Draughtsman, Tom Coleman, after Stanier had departed on a working trip to India in autumn 1936. The CME returned to England in March 1937; two months later, Coronation was completed at Crewe, and on 29th June, the new loco (numbered 6220) and her carriage set were given a promotional run from Euston to Crewe, during which they equalled the 112½ mph reached by the LNER's Silver Link; a reading from Coronation's onboard speed recording device, indicating that a maximum of 114 mph had been reached, was not corroborated by the timekeepers.

Despite her failure to break the British top speed record, Coronation and her siblings delivered splendid levels of performance for the LMS and its passengers, but it was Sir Nigel Gresley (knighted in 1936) and the LNER that were to win themselves an indelible place in the history books for the unmatched velocity of their engines.

On 27th August 1936, the A4 Pacific *Silver Fox* clocked 113 mph with a seven-coach, passenger-carrying southbound train on the 1 in 264 falling gradient between Essendine and Tallington in Lincolnshire, though it sustained considerable mechanical damage as a result, and its crew were, as O S Nock put it, 'adjectively lucky to be able to continue… into King's Cross'. The ultimate honours for high-speed running, though, belong to the LNER's famous *Mallard*, an A4 whose capabilities had been boosted by an upgrade, carried out early in 1938, that replaced the single chimney previously fitted as standard to the class with a Kylchap-style double blastpipe. To quote locomotive expert David Clarke, this 'gave a very distinctive soft exhaust but was highly effective in reducing back pressure'.

Stoke Bank was chosen as the location for a special test trip, involving *Mallard* and a seven-coach, 236½-ton train, including a dynamometer car, scheduled for 3rd July 1938. It was officially announced as a brake trial; but, according to a detailed account published five days later in the *Railway Gazette*, 'in the course of a series of runs between Peterborough and Grantham, it was [also] decided to ascertain the maximum speed of which the engine was capable with this load'. On one of these, the train steadily increased its velocity from 24 mph at Grantham station to 74½ mph on the climb to Stoke Summit, before beginning a serious attempt on the existing records over the falling gradient ahead. Within 6 miles, as Driver Duddington kept his regulator full open and his cut-off at 40%, 116 mph had been reached. Increasing the cut-off to 45% added an extra 3 mph, and then – with the control once again at 40% – *Mallard* accelerated to over 120 mph, attaining a maximum of 125 mph near the milepost marking 90¼ miles from London (though 126 mph is widely claimed, most noticeably on the plaque attached to the engine). This top speed – beating the previous world record of 124½ mph set by the streamlined, Borsig-built German engine 05 002 between Hamburg and Berlin on May 11th 1936 – remains officially unmatched by any other steam locomotive to this day.

WORLD WAR II LOOMS

To aid visibility during blackout, shunting buffers were painted white. The lamps were also hooded to prevent them being seen from above. Photo taken 18th October 1939.

ABOVE
Evacuees leaving Liverpool Street station in 1939.

In September 1938, with Nazi Germany's territorial designs on the Sudetenland region of Czechoslovakia leading to growing international tension, the British government took the first steps towards putting its railways on a war footing. It was decided that, in the event of hostilities, the Great Western, Southern, London Midland & Scottish, and London & North Eastern railways, as well as the London Passenger Transport Board (LPTB), would be brought under the direct control of the Ministry of Transport. An enabling act was not introduced immediately, but a Railway Executive Committee was established on 24th September; it comprised the chief executives of the Big Four and the LPTB, and was tasked with co-ordinating wartime train operations in the national interest, and advising the MoT on a wide range of railway policy matters.

The signing of the Munich Agreement five days later averted the prospect of immediate conflict, but over the following months, the REC, chaired by Sir Ralph Wedgwood of the LNER, was assiduous in preparing for a war that many now considered inevitable. One of its principal concerns was the protection of trains, passengers and the permanent way itself against air raids, especially at night, when brightly illuminated passenger carriages, signal lamps and even the glow from steam locomotives' fireboxes would be dangerously visible to enemy planes. In wartime, residential areas, businesses, road traffic and individual households were all to be subject to 'blackout' conditions between the hours of dusk and dawn, but applying these to the railways was especially difficult and potentially hazardous; in the absence of adequate station lighting, members of the public could (and, later, did) fall from platforms on to the tracks, while staff dispatching trains might fail to spot open carriage doors or people still trying to board.

Various ways were found to maximise the blackout without excessively compromising safety and convenience: colour-light signals were hooded, blue low-wattage bulbs were fitted to coaches, and steam-locomotive cabs were enveloped in anti-glare sheets, which had the regrettable sideeffect of raising footplate temperatures to uncomfortable levels. The efficacy of these measures was put to the test during August 1939, when several trial blackouts, monitored from the air by the RAF, were imposed across various parts of the country; and on 1st September, a night-time blackout was introduced throughout Britain.

The same day as the German invasion of Poland that was to trigger World War II began, the Government invoked the Emergency Powers (Defence) Act, passed on 24th August 1939, and issued an order taking over the railways, whose day-to-day running was to be delegated to the Railway Executive Committee. The 1st September also marked the start of the long-planned evacuation of children and some adults (including expectant mothers, hospital patients and the disabled) from London and other areas considered to be at high risk from air attack. Ships and buses played their part in this massive operation, but the brunt of it was borne by the railway network, which, between 1st and 4th September, carried over 1,300,000 people to towns and villages in the safer parts of the country, termed 'reception areas'.

Most of the evacuees were children, whose parents were instructed to send them to school on the morning of their departure equipped with a gas mask, a change of socks and underwear, night clothes, some basic toiletries, a packed lunch, and, if possible, a warm coat or mackintosh. At school, teachers issued the boys and girls with stamped postcards, which would be used later to notify parents of their offsprings' new addresses, and the children were tagged with name and destination labels. They were then led or driven off to their places of departure; in London, the Underground took many of them to central termini such as Waterloo and Paddington, or to suburban tube/rail stations such as Ealing Broadway and Wimbledon, where they boarded trains – which had been taken out of regular service specially – to convey them to their designated reception areas; despite considerable efforts to place children as close to home as possible, their new billets were sometimes hundreds of miles away.

The evacuation caused temporary disruption to the standard schedules; the Southern Railway gave advance warning that, outside rush-hour periods on 1st–4th September, its 'suburban and main-line [trains would] be cut down to about half of the normal running', and the London Passenger Transport Board announced that 'at certain stations', there would be times during the same four days when 'facilities will be used almost wholly for the conveyance of children, so that it may not be possible to accept ordinary passengers'.

Nevertheless, there were widespread plaudits for the way the railways accomplished their huge task, with *The Times* going so far as to claim that 'no great movement has ever been better executed... Most trains ran to time, every [evacuated] child had a seat, [and] there was no confusion either on departure or arrival'. It went on to acknowledge, rather more realistically, that 'in one or two instances trains arrived at the wrong destinations, but the children were quickly put on the right road'. Such upbeat

assessments (echoed, a few days later, in a radio broadcast by the Minister of Transport, Captain Euan Wallace, who described the handling of the evacuation by railway and bus companies as 'beyond all praise, and in keeping with the splendid traditions of the transport services') were at least partly intended to bolster public morale. However, more recent accounts of the evacuation have been less favourable: *Prisoners of War*, H V Nicholson's fiercely critical study of the subject, published in 2000, states that 'the trains [provided for evacuees] were overcrowded, sometimes without lavatories and with inadequate water supplies, so children arrived tired... dirty and fed up'. However, the railways' success in ferrying so many young passengers in such extraordinary conditions without accident or even serious mishap remains a remarkable logistical achievement.

At the same time as the first evacuees were being moved, a threeday operation, involving 22 special trains, was under way to carry 10,000 men – described in Robert Bell's *History of the British Railways during the War, 1939–45* as 'reinforcements to bring Mediterranean and overseas garrisons up to wartime strength, together with officers and civilians occupying key posts, who were returning from leave' – from the south and west of England to King George V Dock in Glasgow. Mobilisation of Army reservists also took place in advance of Prime Minister Neville Chamberlain's declaration of war on 3rd September,

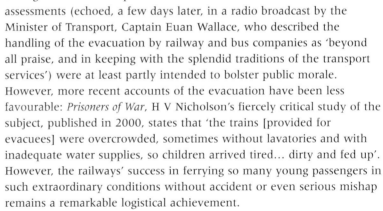

ABOVE
A small boy wonders what the future holds as he is evacuated, 1942.

LEFT
Another scene at London's Liverpool Street station in 1939 as young children are evacuated.

though, according to railway historian Norman Crump, 'in this case no special trains were run'; instead, men were 'given free warrants and travelled by the ordinary train service' to barracks and mustering points.

A far more daunting challenge facing the railways in the early weeks of World War II was the transportation of the British Expeditionary Force, comprising 102,000 troops, and vast tonnages of baggage and weaponry (including 6-in howitzers) to Southampton docks between 9th September and 5th October. For security reasons, no mention of the BEF's movements prior to its departure were published in the contemporary press, and some of the 261 trains carrying its personnel and supplies were obliged to take circuitous routes in order to avoid crossing London, which was thought to be under imminent threat of enemy bombardment.

Such heavy military demands were soon to lead to drastic cutbacks in civilian railway services. Cheap day tickets had been withdrawn at the outbreak of war; simultaneously, several long-distance expresses were suspended or had their speed curtailed; and on Friday 8th September, the LNER, LMS and SR (though not the GWR) announced the introduction, from the following Monday, of emergency timetables, which, as Robert Bell put it, 'reduced most of the weekday main-line services to the level [of a] pre-war Sunday… and limited start-to-stop speeds to 45 mph, with a maximum of 60 mph between stations'. These were combined with cuts in sleeping car provision, and the removal of all restaurant cars, although the companies assured hungry travellers that 'arrangements are being made for "snack boxes" to be available at the more important stations'. On Saturday 9th, the Southern attempted to forestall protests by conceding that 'overcrowding might result' from the new arrangements, and promised that 'the loading of the trains will be watched and adjustments made wherever possible'.

1938

24th September – Railway Executive Committee established

29th September – Munich Agreement signed

1939

24th August – Emergency Powers (Defence) Act passed, enabling Minister of Transport to take control of railways and other key services in a time of national emergency

1st September – railways placed under Government control; nighttime blackout imposed throughout Britain; evacuation of children and some adults from London and other areas at high risk of enemy attack begins; transportation of approximately 10,000 troops and other personnel to Glasgow docks begins

3rd September – war declared

After World War I, gas attacks were feared and everyone was required to carry a gas mask.

Commuter travel on Monday 11th September – and for the rest of the week – was predictably miserable, and on Tuesday 12th, *The Times* carried a graphic account of the previous day's journey into London aboard a jam-packed constantly stopping LNER service, which passengers vainly struggled to board at the busy stations nearest the capital: 'The guard informed those [waiting] on the platforms that there was no room, and added the not very comforting assurance that there would soon be another train. Even allowing an hour for a [trip] that normally takes little more than half an hour, [we were] a quarter of an hour late at King's Cross.'

As customer complaints mounted, the three companies introduced an 'amplification' of their schedules in the week beginning Monday 18th September (when the GWR brought in its own wartime timetable), and by Wednesday 20th, Captain Wallace, the Minister of Transport, was able to report to the House of Commons that the situation regarding scheduling had 'progressively improved during the past 10 days,' with a considerable number of additional passenger trains, particularly in suburban areas. Matters were further ameliorated by the welcome reintroduction of cheap day tickets from 9th October, and the easing of speed limits, plus the reappearance of some restaurant cars a week later. Permanent wartime timetables were in place on all four main networks by February 1940. The prevailing mood on the railways (and throughout the country) at the opening of the war was one of anxiety and uncertainty, tempered with stoicism and resolve. There was little to be light-hearted about, but one newspaper story published in September 1939 would surely have raised a smile from contemporary readers, and casts a touchingly human light on the grim events of the time. It describes the problem faced by the London Passenger Transport Board's lost property office, which, within a few weeks of the outbreak of war, was being inundated with mislaid gas masks, items that were supposed to be carried by adults and children at all times. The nearly 2,000 unclaimed masks in London Transport's possession could not be returned to their rightful owners, as they had not been properly labelled – as required by officialdom – with full names and addresses, but carried only Christian names… or were marked simply 'Mum', 'Dad' and 'Sis'. How many more would there be on LT's shelves before 1945?

75% GOODS
PEACE TIME
25%

SOUTHERN RAILWAY

60%
WAR TIME
40%
FOOD AND WAR SUPPLIES

THIS IS WHY PASSENGER TRAINS HAVE TO BE FEWER AND SLOWER

ABOVE
Poster produced for the SR to explain to passengers that there would be fewer and slower trains during the war.

4th September –
evacuation completed

9th September – 5th October
– British Expeditionary Force and its equipment transported by train to Southampton

11th September –
Railway speed restrictions introduced; restaurant-car facilities withdrawn; emergency schedules on Southern, London Midland & Scottish and London & North Eastern railways drastically reduce passenger services (Great Western amends its timetables a week later)

18th September –
Southern Railway restores many of the services cut the previous week; other companies make similar 'amplifications' to their wartime schedules over the next few days

16th October –
Railway speed restrictions eased; some restaurant cars reinstated

BRITISH STEAM RAILWAYS

PICTURE CREDITS

Horizon International Images Limited / Alamy Stock Photo: cover; Geoff Oliver / Alamy Stock Photo: cover; AKG Images: 7bl, 58tr; P Chancellor Collection: 49br, 50bl, 51tr, 52br; Cody Images: 63tl; Corbis: 20tr; Corbis: Hulton Deutsch: 42br; Getty Images: 42tl, 56bl, 59, 60tl, 61tr; Guildhall Library, City of London: 44bl; Horizon International Images Limited/Alamy Stock Photo: cover l; Hulton Archive: 10 tl, 15tl, 16br; Hulton-Deutsch: 62tl; John Law: 39b; Mike Lee: 47t, 48t; Lynton-Lynmouth Cliff Railway: 49tl; Alexander W V Mace/Milepost 9½: 7 bl; Mary Evans Picture Library: 39bl, 57tl; Medway Archives & Local Studies: 40tr; Milepost 92½: 6t, 7br, 29b, 30t, 32tl, 33br, 36tl; Mirrorpix: 61bl; Michael Morant: 41b; The Museum of the Great Western Railway 54b, 55t; The National Archives Image Library (Public Records Office): 23b; National Portrait Gallery: 20bl; Geoff Oliver/Alamy Stock Photo; David Pollack: 17tl: cover r; Rex Features: Everett Collection: 22tr; Science & Society Picture Library: National Railway Museum 5b, 11t, 12 tl & br, 13 tr & br, 14, 15br, 17c, 16, 20cr, 21tr, 24, 26bl, 27 tl & b, 28tl, 30bl, 31bl, 37b, 40bl, 43b, 45tr, 57br, 63tr; Courtesy of David Shepherd: 46br; www.southern-images.co.uk; 45bl; The Transport Archive: 28br.

Although every effort has been made to trace all picture sources, we regret that in some cases this has not been possible and apologise for any omissions.